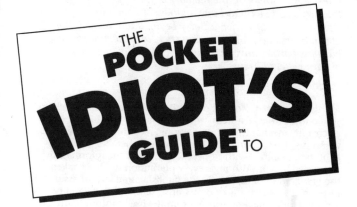

THE POCKET IDIOT'S GUIDE TO

Choosing Cigars

by Tad Gage

alpha books

A Division of Macmillan Reference
A Simon and Schuster Macmillan Company
1633 Broadway, New York, NY 10019-6785

I dedicate this book to the memory of three special people:
Industry giant Herman Lane, founder of Lane Limited, who I
was proud to call a friend. Barry Levin, a tobacconist, honor-
able businessman, industry maverick, and the best friend and
business partner anyone could have. And my mom, who
always believed in me.

©1999 by Tad Gage

THE POCKET IDIOT'S GUIDE TO name and design are registered trademarks of Macmillan.

Macmillan Publishing books may be purchased for business or sales promotional use. For information please write: Special Markets Department, Macmillan Publishing USA, 1633 Broadway, New York, NY 10019.

International Standard Book Number: 0-02-862701-6

Library of Congress Catalog Card Number: 98-88159

01 00 99   8 7 6 5 4 3 2 1

Interpretation of the printing code: the rightmost number of the first series of numbers is the year of the book's printing; the rightmost number of the second series of numbers is the number of the book's printing. For example, a printing code of 99-1 shows that the first printing occurred in 1999.

Printed in the United States of America

Note: This publication contains the opinions and ideas of its author. It is intended to provide helpful and informative material on the subject matter covered. It is sold with the understanding that the author and publisher are not engaged in rendering professional services in the book. If the reader requires personal assistance or advice, a competent professional should be consulted.

The author and publisher specifically disclaim any responsibility for any liability, loss or risk, personal or otherwise, which is incurred as a consequence, directly or indirectly, of the use and application of any of the contents of this book.

Contents

Introduction

Cigars can seem intimidating, especially if you're standing in a shop, toe-to-toe with dozens of cedar boxes filled with countless cigars. This can be daunting, but it's also the beginning of an adventure. With a keen eye, a discriminating palate, and enough knowledge, you can find your prize. I'd love to help guide you.

I frequently draw comparisons between wine and cigars. In many ways, they're a lot alike—from the care and skill needed to make a fine product, to the fact that the more you learn, the more fun you'll have. As with wine, you can jump right in and start enjoying cigars. With time and experience, you'll gain a greater appreciation of what you like and why you like it.

How to Use This Book

Whether you've never smoked a cigar before or you've enjoyed a lot of stogies and want to know more, you can use this book to enhance your cigar experience. I've designed this book to help guide you on your own adventure through the world of cigars: A place where you can own and consume a bit of lore and legend, relax in your own private world of warm tropical breezes, and enjoy a flavor sensation unlike anything else on earth.

In this book, you'll learn how to:

➤ Speak the language of cigars

➤ Identify a potentially great smoke on sight

➤ Quickly weed out "wannabe" cigars that are premium in price only

➤ Make good cigar-buying decisions at all price points

If you want a no-nonsense approach to understanding cigars, this book is for you! It provides all the basic knowledge you need to start enjoying cigars: Where to find them; how to talk about them; and how to select, cut, and light them. Heck, you don't have to know *everything* to enjoy a great cigar, so light up and start reading!

You'll also learn what makes an attractive visual presentation, how to judge a cigar by looks (and labels), and how you can make sure you get your money's worth.

Extras

Along the way, you'll find tips and tidbits that will help you more fully enjoy cigars:

Hot Tip

These snippets of red-hot information help guide you through the world of cigars.

Blowing Smoke

These cautions highlight important, more involved facts you should know about cigars and tobacco, and how to cut through the smoke and mirrors to find the truth about cigars.

Cigar Speak

These definitions will help you talk about cigars like an aficionado.

Acknowledgments

I'd like to thank the cigar manufacturers who hung in there during the industry's tough times, and who supported me and my magazine. Thanks to cigar manufacturers Paul Garmirian and the Fuente family, retailers Diana Gits of Up Down Tobacco and Chuck Levi of Iwan Ries, Harry Kuchma (my guide through the world of spirits), and my Alpha Books editors for their assistance, cooperation, and enthusiastic support in making this book a reality. Thanks to Susan Ireland for introducing me to the *Pocket Idiot's* series, and Andrèe Abecassis, an agent and friend. Also, I appreciate the contributions of my knowledgeable technical editor, Tony Palacios, the epitome of a tobacconist.

Extra special thanks to my cigar-loving wife Cyndi, who was so helpful and supportive during this process that I married her.

Special Thanks to the Technical Editor

The Pocket Idiot's Guide to Choosing Cigars was reviewed by an expert in the field who not only checked the technical accuracy of everything you'll learn here, but also provided insight to help us ensure that this book tells you everything you need to know about cigars. Our special thanks are extended to Anthony Palacios.

Tony has more than 20 years experience in the retail tobacco business. He began as a stock clerk at Iwan Ries &

Company (IRC), and was groomed by Stanley Levi, who built IRC into one of the largest and most prominent tobacconists in the country. Now in its 140th year, this multimillion dollar, family-owned business is run by fourth generation Charles S. Levi. Tony serves as vice president.

Tony has been intimately involved with the development and sales of the respected IRC house cigar brands and actively promoted the growth in cigar popularity long before the current cigar explosion. He has participated in and hosted numerous cigar events, and has total familiarity with today's wide range of cigar brands.

Chapter 1

Appreciating a Good Cigar

I, like everyone else, started out as a cigar idiot. I was 25 years old, and I had never smoked *anything*. It was the fall of 1982, and I was in Toronto attending a financial and banking conference. After dinner, each attendee was presented with a tubed H. Upmann Cuban cigar.

When the speeches were done, I retired to my room. I struck the match and raised the flame to the cigar. I was lucky that I'd never smoked before, because my throat instantly closed, not allowing me to inhale the smoke, but simply to roll it around in my mouth and gently let the smoke drift out. Leaning back in my chair, I drew long, luxurious draughts of this magical cylinder. I smoked it to the stub, which is what I do, to this day, with a really good cigar. I tasted flavors unlike anything I had ever experienced.

Like me, I hope you become passionate about a good cigar. Enjoying a smoke in the privacy of my home gives me time to kick back and contemplate the day—or maybe think about nothing at all. When I light up with my cigar-loving friends, we have a chance to talk, laugh, swap stories, and rate our smokes.

Fire Away!

To appreciate a good cigar, you don't need anything more than a good smoke and perhaps a few good friends. I'd like you to start enjoying cigars right away, while you're reading this book. A knowledge of cigars and tobacco definitely enhances your puffing pleasure, but you don't have to wait until you're an expert to grab a stogie and light up!

Smoking cigars, like enjoying wine, should be fun! There's a world of information and knowledge you can use to enhance your enjoyment, but you can also have great experiences with cigars no matter what "level" you're at. Discovering new brands and new flavors is an adventure, and with each new smoke, you'll add to your storehouse of knowledge.

So, how simple is it to get started? Here's all you need:

➤ A handmade cigar (about $3 to $10)

➤ A box of wooden matches or a disposable butane lighter (about $1)

➤ An inexpensive guillotine-style clipper (you can buy one from many cigar retailers for about $2, or you can have the dealer clip your cigar)

➤ An ashtray

➤ About 45 minutes to kick back and relax

A Basic Sampling

So, what cigar should you smoke? If you've already smoked a few (or more than a few) cigars, you may have some favorites. Most retailers will be able to present you with a selection of handmade smokes—the kind you should insist on buying.

If you've never smoked premium handmade cigars, the selection at a well-stocked shop can be a little intimidating. If you're just starting out and you want to try a few different cigars, think about buying three sizes: a short, thick cigar (commonly called a *robusto*); a mid-sized cigar (a *corona* size—about 5 inches long); and a longer, larger cigar such as a *double corona* (about 7 inches long).

This selection will give you a little variety and the chance to test out the smoking qualities of three cigars—each with a different feel and taste.

Cigar Speak

Cigars are classified by their length and girth. Three examples are the **robusto** (short and thick); the mid-sized **corona** (moderately slim and in the middle of the cigar-length spectrum); and the **double corona**—sometimes called a **Churchill** (which is long and relatively thick).

What brands should you select? You want to start off with mild, well-made cigars; they'll give you a good smoke and they're the easiest for a beginner to appreciate. In Chapter 6, I talk about how you can progress from mild to wild.

Nationally available brands that combine quality and mildness are Macanudo, Don Diego, Temple Hall, Cuesta Rey, Baccarrat, Montesino, and Royal Jamaica. Most of these are also a good value—about $2 to $9. If you can't find *any* of these brands, ask the retailer for some recommendations.

In Chapter 8, you'll find a sample rating sheet with room for a lot of detail. Feel free to use all or part of it when you're starting out on your adventure.

Until you have a *humidor* (a place in which to store your cigars and keep them moist and flavorful), you can keep a handful of stogies in a plastic storage container. (Buy a new one at the grocery store; don't use one that has stored food because it may give your cigars a funny taste.) You can also use a tight-sealing bag or box.

Cigar Speak

A **humidor** is an enclosed device that keeps cigars in a tropical climate. A humidor can be a walk-in room, a box made of wood or Plexiglas, or a sealed plastic bag—anything that maintains the humidity cigars require to keep from drying out.

Luck of "The Draw"

You know a cigar is handmade if one end is completely sealed and has to be clipped off in order to draw any air through the cigar. Drawing air through the cigar is called, appropriately, *the draw,* and it is one of the most important aspects of smoking and enjoying a cigar.

Clipping a cigar is almost an art form in itself, and you have many options for how to clip a cigar. Chapter 3 talks about how to clip your cigar. Most places that sell cigars will clip them for you, which is a good option until you purchase a cutter.

Cigar Speak

A **cutter** is a device used to remove the sealed tip of a cigar, which allows you to draw air through the cigar. Numerous types and several styles of cutters are available.

Of course, you can't test the draw by clipping the end and putting it in your mouth before you light up! Instead, your best bet is to buy well-known brands from manufacturers who take pride in turning out tens of thousands of perfectly crafted cigars. (Later in this chapter, you'll find a list of your best-bet brands.)

If you buy a cigar from a retailer, light it up right there, and discover that you're having a problem drawing air through the cigar (and you'll know after a puff or two), tell the retailer. Many times, the merchant will replace your cigar free of charge. For a retailer who wants your continued patronage, this courtesy is a very small cost of doing business.

Anatomy of a Cigar

Especially now that cigars are trendy, it helps to have a little knowledge right from the start. Understanding what contributes to a good cigar is delightfully complex, but we'll start off easy. The cigar itself is pretty simple. The following illustration sums it up.

The anatomy of a cigar.

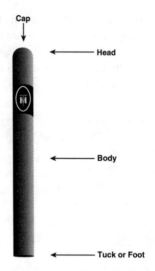

Cap

Head

Body

Tuck or Foot

You'll learn a lot more detail when I discuss how a cigar is constructed in Chapter 6, but for now, here are the basics:

➤ **Filler** Long leaves of tobacco or cut up pieces of tobacco that comprise the bulk of the cigar and deliver most of the flavor.

➤ **Binder** Tough, coarse tobacco that holds the whole thing together.

➤ **Wrapper** A silky leaf of tobacco that makes your cigar look and feel attractive.

➤ **Cap** or **head** Offers a nice appearance and, if applied properly, feels good in your mouth and prevents the wrapper from unraveling.

➤ **Foot** The business end of the cigar—the end that you light.

Grab Your Wallet: What You'll Pay

What can you expect to fork over for the simple pleasure of a fine cigar? A lot of what you pay depends on where you make your purchase. (I'll talk more about the different places to purchase cigars in Chapter 2.) The good news is that a lot of great smokes are out there if you know what to look for. The bad news is that you can also find some mediocre smokes at some very high prices. Price doesn't always indicate quality, but until you have the knowledge to make a fully educated decision, try to stick with name brands and accept the going rate, which will probably average $5 to $8 for a medium-sized cigar.

In a cigar bar or restaurant, expect the kind of markup on cigars that you'd expect on wine or liquor—about two to three times more than you'd pay at a shop. It's tough to find a decent cigar in a bar or restaurant for less than $8. You can drop as much as $25 for a really fine cigar, but chalk it up to the cost of not bringing your own. Add it to the $38 bottle of wine you can find at the wine shop for $10.99!

In a well-stocked smoke shop, or at a liquor retailer with a decent humidor, you can probably find a nice handmade cigar (one of the smaller sizes) for around $2.50. Larger, longer cigars, like Churchills, cost more because they're harder to make and they use more tobacco. Smaller cigars, like robustos or petite coronas, will cost less than larger cigars in the same line.

Today, you can find cigars at $25 each and higher, while some boxes of 25 may cost anywhere from $800 to $1,000. You don't have to spend anywhere near this much to get a great smoke, but if your budget allows you to experiment with some of these pricey stogies, go ahead. Remember: You can find some super smokes for $3 or $4, with boxes of 25 costing $70 to $100.

Hot Tip

If you want to buy a box (and you should, if you can find a box of a cigar that you like), expect to pay anywhere from $70 to $250 for a box of 25 super-premium, handmade cigars, depending on size and brand.

If you're trying a particular brand for the first time (and you don't have an unlimited budget), buy a smaller, less expensive cigar. The taste and quality of a smaller cigar will be representative of larger cigars in the same line; if you don't like the cigar, you've wasted a lot less money when you drop it in the ashtray!

I recommend selecting established, well-known brands. A lot of new handmade brands are coming on the market, but the reality is that their quality is not up to snuff. Some good new brands are popping up, but often the makers simply don't have access to good leaf. Your best bet for a great smoke is to find an established brand with a track record of quality and consistency.

By now you might be asking: "What are the well-known brands?" Well, hold on a minute and I'll give you a cheat sheet to start you off. In Chapters 9 through 12, I've listed more extensive descriptions of many of these brands by price. This listing should help in your selection and give you something to compare against your perceptions.

What's in a Name?

Here's a listing, in alphabetical order, of cigar brands that have been around a while and whose makers have an established reputation for quality construction and tobacco. To help make your hunt easier, I've only included private-label or store brands that are sold through numerous retail outlets.

Because Cuban cigars aren't legally available in the U.S., I haven't included any of them in this list. Most Cuban brands have a non-Cuban counterpart—in name only; not even the smallest amount of Cuban tobacco is allowed in cigars legally exported to the United States.

- ➤ Arturo Fuente, Ashton, Avo Uvezian
- ➤ Baccarrat, Bances, Bauza, Belinda, Bering, Butera
- ➤ Canaria D'Oro, Juan Clemente, Credo, Cuba Aliados, Cuesta Rey
- ➤ Davidoff, Diana Silvius, Don Diego, Don Juan, Don Tomas, Dunhill
- ➤ El Rey del Mundo, El Sublimado
- ➤ Fonseca
- ➤ Griffin's
- ➤ Henry Clay, Thomas Hinds, H. Upmann, Hoyo de Monterrey
- ➤ Joya de Nicaragua, Jose Llopis
- ➤ Licenciados, La Unica
- ➤ Macanudo, Montesino, Montecruz
- ➤ Nat Sherman
- ➤ Onyx, Oscar
- ➤ PG (Paul Garmirian), Partagas, Petrus, Pleiades, Por Larranaga, Primo del Rey, Punch, Punch Gran Cru
- ➤ Ramon Allones, Romeo y Julieta, Royal Jamaica
- ➤ Santa Clara, Santa Damiana, Sosa, Savinelli
- ➤ Te Amo, Temple Hall, Troya
- ➤ Zino

If you like a good deal, your head will turn when a cigar retailer shows you a great-looking no-name cigar that's half the price of the name brands. And you just may have found a great deal!

Many shop retailers and direct-mail sellers offer un-branded, handmade premium cigars. There's usually no cigar band on these smokes. Sometimes these are sold in bundles of 10 or 25, and often singly, as well. There are two kinds of no-name smokes:

➤ *Seconds* are cigars that have been rejected by a major manufacturer because they have flaws that make them unacceptable to sell as branded "firsts." A maker of super-premium stogies might reject a cigar for something as picky as a color flaw or spots on the wrapper. Sometimes a cigar will have a soft spot—maybe the roller had a bad day—and will be rejected. You will learn later more about why soft spots are not acceptable in premium cigars, and how they affect your smoke.

➤ *Bundles* are usually cigars that were made to sell as no-name smokes, but they can also be stogies that a retailer got at a special price. A manufacturer, for example, might have had an overrun on a certain size, or perhaps ran out of boxes. Typically, you'll see a group of 25 cigars called "Dominican Bundle" or "Honduran Bundle" indicating the country of origin. Bundles can be a one-time deal, or the retailer might have an ongoing order for these no-name smokes.

Cigar Speak

The **band** is a colorful strip of paper applied around the cigar, usually near the head, that identifies the maker. It's the only mark a cigar manufacturer can use to identify individual cigars as his product.

Why should you bother with unbranded cigars? Because if you get lucky you can get a great deal on a great smoke! For about half the price of a branded, banded cigar, you can get a cigar that's almost as good. Despite visual flaws or soft spots, many unbranded cigars usually feature the same tobacco and the same quality construction as branded cigars. (Be aware, however, that a no-name cigar might have a major flaw, such as being rolled so tightly that you can't draw air through it. You take your chances with a no-name cigar.)

If you can buy a no-name stogie for around half the price of a name brand, get one, fire it up, and see what you think. What have you got to lose? If you like it and you can live with its flaws, buy a few more; because it's a reject, it may be the first, last, and only time that you'll find that particular cigar!

Retailers who are extremely well-connected with manufacturers may sell their own brand of cigars made by one of the major manufacturers. These cigars can range from dirt cheap to pricey, but they'll generally be less expensive than major brands because the retailer buys a regular allotment and the boxes, labels, and advertising all cost less for these cigars. If you're budget-conscious, or you just want to find a good "everyday" smoke at a very reasonable price, check out these options. Because you don't have a brand name to go by, the only way to know whether you like a particular cigar carried by a retailer is to try one.

Lighting Up: It's a Gas

Getting started with cigars is pretty easy, and one simple trick can greatly improve your smoking pleasure: When you light up (using only wooden matches or a butane lighter; I'll explain why in Chapter 3), hold the cigar gently in your mouth and turn it slowly as you let the flame kiss the end of the cigar.

Draw in air using slow, gentle puffs. If you're chugging away like a steam locomotive, you're pulling too much air in and the cigar will get hot. It takes a few seconds to light your cigar using this gentle puffing, turning technique.

Check the end to make sure that the entire tip is glowing. If there's a part that isn't, return the cigar to your mouth and hold the flame to that section for just a second. Then take the flame away to avoid catching the wrapper on fire. If it does, blow out the flame and let the cigar "settle down" for a moment before you start enjoying it!

Check the tip again for an even light. If it needs just a little more help, blow lightly on it to fan the glowing tip. Then let your cigar rest for a few seconds before you take that first luxurious puff.

Following this technique allows your cigar to get off to a good start; you've done everything possible to ensure that the cigar will burn evenly. If left unattended, your cigar will burn for about three to five minutes.

For some smokers, it's a mark of power and confidence to jam a big cigar between their molars and puff jauntily away. A better way to enjoy the full flavor and experience of a cigar is to "sip" it by placing it to your lips—not between your teeth—and pulling in a deep and satisfying draught. Let your cigar rest for 30 seconds to a minute between puffs. Your smoke will be cooler, and because it's not crammed in your mouth, people will be able to understand you when you talk.

Cigars are meant to be sipped and savored, but not inhaled. The key to enjoying cigar smoke is to draw the smoke in, let it swirl around your mouth, savor it like fine wine, and release it gently from your mouth.

Hot Tip

You should always "sip" your cigar, not jam it between your teeth and puffing away. Sipping your cigar will keep the head of your cigar relatively dry; holding it in your mouth will cause you to salivate, which will make your smoke soggy and produce bitter, tarry juice that will mar the quality of your smoke.

Unlike cigarettes, which will burn down to the filter if left unpuffed, cigar tobacco is too moist to burn without oxygen (provided by you). Most cigarettes also contain chemical additives that promote burning, while tobacco in handmade cigars contains no additives. (As with all rules, this one has an exception: A few brands are accented with a light flavor base and do contain additives.) If your cigar goes out, gently knock the excess ash off the tip and relight it using the same technique as when you started.

Hot Tip

Never chew or chomp a premium cigar; instead, you should hold it in your hand or place it in an ashtray. Smoking stimulates saliva, so if you hold the cigar in your mouth, it will start to get soggy, clogging the air hole and ruining the draw.

Where Can You Smoke?

As you puff your way through the exciting world of cigars, you'll probably begin to discover times or places when having a cigar seems especially appropriate. Keep in mind that unless you smoke outside, or you live alone, or light up in your own home with no spouse or kids or room-mates around, you'll be sharing your passion for cigars with others—and sometimes they'd rather you didn't. Remember that part of smoking is being considerate.

It's best to smoke a cigar inside: A breeze can make your stogie burn hot and fast. If, however, your best chance to smoke is on your porch, out on the golf course, or while taking a walk, by all means go ahead and enjoy! You can smoke in the car, but it's a challenge to drive and properly savor a cigar at the same time.

If nobody minds you smoking at home, you're in good shape. If, however, you're not ready to jump over that hurdle, several indoor options are still open to you:

➤ Visit one of the growing number of cigar bars.

➤ Track down a cigar-friendly restaurant or pub.

➤ Enjoy your cigar right where you bought it; many smoke shops offer seating for customers.

You can frequently track down smoke shops and cigar bars by thumbing through the Yellow Pages. In Chapter 2, you'll read about different places you can buy and smoke cigars.

The Least You Need to Know

➤ Enjoying and experimenting with cigars should be fun.

➤ To be assured of the best consistency and quality, stick with established name brands.

➤ Feel free to try a "no-name" cigar if it's a good deal and you can afford to toss it if you don't like it.

➤ For an even, cool smoke, puff slowly and gently on your cigar, giving it time to rest between puffs.

➤ Be considerate of those around you when you smoke.

Chapter 2

Sniffing Out the Good Stuff

Snf
Snf

In This Chapter

➤ Improving your odds of finding a great smoke in a tight market

➤ Shopping around for a winning cigar retailer

➤ What to expect if you buy a cigar at a bar or restaurant

➤ Tracking down cigars through the mail and the Internet

➤ How to check out and size up a retailer's humidor

These days, it seems as if everybody is selling cigars. Although such a variety and selection is wonderful, the number of people offering smokes means you have to be a good consumer. Even if a cigar looks good, you have no guarantee of the quality of tobaccos used to make it. And a lot of inferior leaf is being rushed into production to capitalize on the cigar craze. This chapter offers some pointers about how to be a good consumer: what to look for, and what to be wary of. Ultimately, the best guide will be your own taste.

Desperately Seeking Cigars

It's not difficult to find cigars today, but it can be a trick to find good ones. I feel ambivalent about the exploding popularity of (preferably *not* exploding) cigars. On one hand, it's great to see an industry I know and respect enjoying new levels of prestige, success, and prosperity. On the other hand, I see a lot of inferior product coming on the market because of the rush to cash in on the popularity of cigars.

A lot of new cigar smokers have probably never tasted a really good cigar. At the same time, a lot of veteran cigar smokers are hopping mad because they can't find any of their favorite brands.

This scarcity will probably continue for at least the next couple years, because the backlog of good cigars is depleted, and each year only a limited amount of premium cigar leaf can be grown and properly aged. You can't just fire up the cigar assembly line and crank out more product at a moment's notice; a fine cigar requires years to complete.

Cigar Speak

Several things distinguish a **tobacconist** from a mere cigar retailer. The tobacconist has a wide selection of brands and sizes; proper humidification for the stock; a strong working knowledge of cigars, tobacco, and brands; and a selection of smoking-related accessories such as cutters, lighters, and humidors.

It's easy to buy cigars. You go to a place that sells them, ask for advice, or just grab a handful. If you find a good tobacconist and work with someone who really knows cigars and tobacco, it can be very easy to find great cigars. That's why I want you to have as much information as possible.

Tobacconist or "Seegar Seller"?

Your mission, should you choose to accept it, is to find a retailer—or several retailers—with connections. Your best bet is to find a smoke shop. You can usually tell a tobacconist (or smoke shop) from a "seegar seller" because a tobacconist sells a variety of tobacco products, including pipes, pipe tobacco, premium cigarettes, cigarillos, and, of course, premium cigars.

Smoke shops are more likely to have what you're looking for, and have more of it. They have better connections. Many shop owners are members of trade associations that provide the shop owners with direct and regular contact with leading manufacturers. Sometimes, the owners get special pricing and products from manufacturers.

Smoke-shop owners tend to buy a larger volume and variety of products, which ties them more closely to companies that distribute premium smoking-related products. All this puts a smoke shop closer to first in line to receive whatever primo cigars are available. When good smokes are as scarce as they are now, you want every advantage you can get.

At an established tobacconist, you're more likely to find assistants who can give you valuable guidance in selecting cigars and smoking accessories. These shops are in business for the long run, and many of their owners believe that paying for and training a good staff is a great investment in customer relations.

A cigar store/club can be a fun place to enjoy a cigar. Many newer cigar stores have developed a "clubby" approach, offering overstuffed chairs, glorious-looking humidors, a limited bar, and possibly even long-term cigar storage in humidified lockers.

You have to be careful when seeking guidance in your cigar selection, however, because many of these establishments are primarily capitalizing on the cigar craze. Many are staffed by people with limited industry contacts, a very spotty selection, and little or no knowledge of cigars.

I apply a very strict standard to anyone selling cigars, and smoke shops generally come closest to my criteria. A store should offer a wide variety of good, premium, and super-premium cigars. In addition, the staff must display at least a limited knowledge of the products being sold.

Spirited Sales: Liquor Stores and Cigar Bars

A relatively new phenomenon is the *cigar bar*. Cigar bars are places that sell a limited selection of cigars; have a nicely stocked bar, comfy chairs, and cozy nooks; and sometimes offer small appetizers.

You might periodically feel like stopping into one of these atmospheric bars and having a cigar. If you don't have your own stogie with you, just walk in, pick a cigar, step to the register, close your eyes, and open your wallet. Then, sink back in that leather couch, fire up, and set aside your cares.

Cigar Speak

A **cigar bar** is a place with comfortable seating and/or tables where you can make individual selections of cigars, and then accompany them with drinks.

One of the most common alternative places to find cigars today is the liquor store. Large chains and liquor super-stores have the volume, buying power, and finances to build humidors and retail premium cigars. Although I've seldom seen a liquor store on a par with a venerable smoke shop, some have set up smoke shops within the store, and may have a reasonably knowledgeable staff. These are your best bets for finding good smokes and valuable guidance.

These stores also often have facilities for properly storing and humidifying the stock—whether it's a cedar-lined room or just a humidified display case. In addition, own-ers have established good contacts with suppliers, which means they're more likely to be closer to the top of the "pecking order" to receive premium cigars when they're available.

Pasta or Cuban Corona? Cigars at Restaurants

As with newly established cigar "clubs" and cigar bars, most restaurants that offer cigars should be viewed as places to pick up a single cigar from time to time. The nice thing about buying a stogie at a cigar-friendly bar or res-taurant is that the staff will clip it for you and you can light up and start enjoying!

Hot Tip

Most restaurants charge you a steep corkage fee if you bring your own wine. But almost all cigar-friendly bars and restaurants—even if they sell cigars—will allow you to bring and smoke your own cigars. I almost always bring my own.

Although only a few restaurants and bars actually sell cigars, there are many cigar-friendly restaurants and bars throughout the United States. A cigar-friendly establishment welcomes you to bring your own and fire up after a hearty meal or with a smooth drink.

Cigars in the Mail, on the Net

You can buy anything through catalogs and direct mail—including cigars. Cigar retailers have conducted very healthy mail-order businesses for years. Because this is the age of electronics, you can now buy cigars through the Internet, too. Your best bet is to buy cigars in person. If, however, you live someplace where it's difficult to find a good supply of cigars locally, or you just want to see what's out there, I heartily encourage you to explore direct mail.

A number of top-notch retailers conduct large mail-order businesses, and many have toll-free numbers and catalogs. By asking knowledgeable cigar-smoking friends, surfing the Internet, or checking cigar magazines, you should be able to track down any number of retailers who offer cigars by mail.

When ordering by phone, tell the merchant the type of handmade cigar you want—size, shape, mild or full-bodied—and let the merchant tell you what's available. With the spotty supply of cigars, you could spend all day making a "wish list" only to find the retailer is out of stock on everything you want!

Explore the Net by firing up your search engine and searching for *cigars*. You'll find Internet cigar chat rooms and bulletin boards, as well as cigar bulletin boards on services such as America Online and CompuServe. A number of smoke shops I know participate in cigar bulletin board activities, and many will ship cigars to you. Because I have "cigar" in the profile section of my online address, I get quite a few e-mails from people selling cigars—most of them telling me they have a great deal for me.

Hot Tip
A reputable mail-order merchant will make every effort to sell only the finest, freshest cigars, and you may have great luck in finding a smoke not available locally! Some merchants will gladly take back cigars and refund your money if you find the quality unacceptable on the first cigar or two. Ask before you buy.

I've never bought cigars through the Internet, so I don't profess to know whether or not it's a good source of supply. Use the same caution in checking out an Internet cigar vendor as you would for any business offering products through the Net.

Lead Me to Your Humidor

Unless you buy cigars by direct mail or through the Net, you'll have the chance to check out the actual product. Let's take a tour of the different storage conditions you're likely to find when you visit your local cigar retailer.

Unless you're in the Caribbean, where the humidity level is naturally perfect, never buy a premium cigar from a retailer of any kind if the cigar isn't kept in a humidified environment. At times you can tell immediately whether a cigar has been stored improperly; at other times, you'll need to do a little detective work.

Most retailers have one of two common humidors—or both. Individual cigars and open boxes are frequently displayed in sealed glass cases, which are kept at the perfect humidity level by water-soaked chunks of florist's foam, bricks of special absorbent clay, or other humidifying elements. These elements are usually hidden, but feel free to ask the retailer how he keeps the cigars in the display case moist and fresh.

Decide for yourself whether a cigar is fresh by applying the *pinch test.* If you're gentle, a retailer won't object. *Lightly* "pinch" the cigar between your thumb and index finger. It should feel firm, but not hard. If it feels like a piece of wood, or if you feel a soft, spongy spot, choose a different cigar from the same box and try again.

Cigar Speak

The **pinch test** is an easy way to check the construction of your cigar. *Lightly* "pinch" the cigar between your thumb and index finger. It should feel firm, but not hard. If it feels like a piece of wood, or if you feel a spongy spot, choose a different cigar.

The pinch test is the easiest way to tell whether the retailer is properly humidifying the cigars. Glass cases are good for displaying cigars, but they aren't ideal for long-term storage because they're constantly being opened and closed as customers make selections. Consequently, it's tough to maintain proper conditions.

In smaller smoke shops, or those with limited display space, individual cigars are frequently displayed in glass cases, while unopened boxes are kept in a humidified room. You may not be able to check out this room for yourself, but you can judge by the condition of the individually displayed cigars.

Blowing Smoke

If cigars have split wrappers, the retailer may store his stock in an under-humidified room. Moving from a dry room to a humid display case will cause wrappers to split. If customers mishandle the cigars, which can also cause wrappers to break, the retailer is still at fault.

An increasingly common option is for retailers to display boxed and individual cigars in walk-in, cedar-lined humidors, which have strict temperature and humidity controls. Ideally, these rooms also have a ventilation system or at least a fan to keep air circulating. Air movement helps keep mold from developing.

Usually, these rooms are kept moist using room-sized humidifiers. A conscientious retailer will continually monitor the temperature and humidity in the humidor. You may even see gauges. If so, sneak a peek at them: They should register close to 70 percent relative humidity and 70° Fahrenheit.

Some retailers have large humidors, but they don't allow customers inside. You stand outside and make your selection by viewing displayed cigars through a glass window or a sliding glass door. Sometimes retailers do this because the humidor is too small to accommodate many customers. Other times, it's because the retailer is concerned that proper humidity won't be maintained as customers constantly enter and exit the humidor.

These are both very good reasons to keep customers out, but not being able to go into the humidor *does* make selecting the perfect cigar a little more difficult. Ask your sales assistant to bring out a full (opened) box of the brand and size you want so that you can pick out the best-looking cigar of the bunch. Remember the pinch test!

Blowing Smoke

Never buy cigars from a retailer who keeps them refrigerated! This used to be fairly common, although fewer retailers now use this method. Some people believe refrigeration keeps cigars fresh, but refrigerators actually dry out a cigar. You won't find a savvy retailer using this technique.

Not only are you more likely to find the nicest cigar, but picking out a cigar from the box is fun. Later, I talk about all the things you can look for to help you identify the perfect cigar, and why these things are important.

When to Walk Away

Right now, as you're starting on your cigar adventure, it's enough to know the following guidelines:

➤ If the cigar wrapper is cracked, *choose another.*

➤ If there's a whitish mold on the cigar, *choose another.*

➤ If the wrapper has green blotches all over it, *choose another.*

➤ If it's rock-hard or has spongy spots when you lightly pinch it, *choose another.*

➤ If it has little holes the size of a pinhead, or little "trails" running through it, *run like heck!*

Little holes in a cigar or little trails carved out in the cigar are signs of a tobacco beetle infestation. Later, we'll talk more about what this means. For now, unless you enjoy the prospect of smoking bugs, your best bet is to avoid making another selection from this box.

Whenever you buy an unopened box of cigars, whether it's stored in a back room or right there in the humidor, ask the retailer to open the box so that you can inspect the cigars before purchasing them. You want to look for the same things you'd look for in a single cigar.

Until you start building more knowledge about cigars, though, stick to buying individual cigars. Buying a box of handmade cigars, like buying a case of wine, is a significant investment. You want to be sure what you're looking for before you take the plunge.

The Least You Need to Know

➤ Make friends with a local tobacconist to have the best chance of finding the cigars you want in today's tight market.

➤ Cigar bars and restaurants are fine for individual cigar selections, but stick with a full-service retailer for better selection and better prices.

➤ Make sure your retailer maintains proper humidity and temperature conditions for the cigars.

➤ Walk away from a retailer selling moldy cigars or stogies with signs of tobacco beetles.

Chapter 3

The Right Tools for the Job

In This Chapter

➤ How to prepare your cigar with the right cut

➤ Selecting the best tool to "light your fire"

➤ Why you should give your cigar a rest in the ashtray

It's time to discover all the tools at your disposal to enjoy your cigar experience—from preparing your prize, to the proper way to light, smoke, and transport your cigars around the block or around the world. Lighters and cutters may seem like minor aspects of the cigar experience. After all, it's the *cigar* you're smoking, right? Not completely.

If you don't have the right tools to get your stogie off to a good start, you're a lot less likely to have the best smoking experience possible. Also, part of enjoying a cigar is the ritual—a subtle art that's lost on many smokers. The tools and gadgets that accompany cigar smoking provide part of the experience, so be prepared to enjoy!

The Cutting Edge

There's a fine and practiced art to preparing your cigar for smoking. The first step is to prepare the head of your cigar. All premium, handmade cigars come with a cap of tobacco (cut from the same leaf as the tobacco used for the cigar wrapper) that requires either cutting or puncturing.

You want to cut or puncture the end of the cigar just enough to create a thick and satisfying draw (which I discussed in Chapter 1), but also leave the cigar as intact as possible. You should feel a slight resistance when you puff, but you shouldn't have to work hard to draw through the cigar.

One thing to remember when considering any cutter: The sharpness of the blade is everything. Any type of cut with a dull blade will tend to mash the head, which could cause the delicate cap to fray, the wrapper to unwind, and bits of the filler tobacco to dislodge into your mouth. With that overriding rule in mind, let's take a look at all the alternatives you have for creating an airhole.

The "V"-Cut

A common and longtime favorite is the *v-cut,* which does exactly what the name implies. It's a top-to-bottom slice that creates a wedge through the head of the cigar. The v-cut goes deeper into the body of the cigar than any other type of cut, yet leaves the two sides fully rounded. By going deeper, it opens more surface area of the filler, creating a large and lush draw.

Cigar Speak

A **v-cut** is a top-to-bottom slice that creates a v-shaped wedge through the head of the cigar.

You'll find handheld v-cutters everywhere—from simple stainless steel cutters to cutters with antler, rosewood, or gold handles to gold- or silver-plated cutters. Generally, handheld v-cutters not only include a v-cutter, but one hole on either side to create a straight cut. They all work pretty much the same—with a spring-loaded lever and a pad for your thumb.

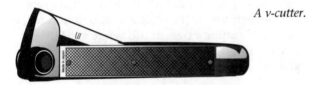

A v-cutter.

Here's how the v-cutter works: An indentation receives the head of the cigar, and holding the cigar in one hand and the cutter in your other hand, press down on the lever and the point of the triangular blade slices through the head of your cigar. Usually the sides of the cutter include two different-sized indentations for making a straight cut. When you use the cutter this way, the sides of the blade snick off the head of the cigar.

V-cutters have one significant problem: I've never seen one with a sharp enough blade. It's difficult to sharpen the blade of a v-cutter, even when it's new, because of the triangular shape. And it's impossible to re-sharpen the blade, because you'd have to break the cutter to get a file onto the blade. Smokers' drawers around the world must be filled with used and discarded v-cutters! I recommend against the handheld v-cutters, but one recommended brand is the Boston cigar cutter, which has very sharp blades.

As with all rules, this one has an exception: the large and heavy table v-cutter. To use this tool, you cut the cigar not by pressing your thumb on a lever, but by applying pressure to a lever that looks similar to an automobile stick shift. Of course, there's no guarantee that the blade will be sharp, but most table models I've seen have a very sharp blade that can be replaced with new blades ordered from the manufacturers.

The two drawbacks to the table model v-cutter are lack of portability and cost. The best ones will run you $350 or more. Granted, they usually sport nice wood and are very effective, but they're impossible to cart around. You can find tabletop v-cutters for as little as $50, but make sure you test the sharpness of the blade and smoothness of the mechanism by cutting a cigar or two before you buy the cutter. Many smoke shops have table v-cutters, however, so if you crave a v-cut, make your cuts at the store.

Prices on handheld v-cutters really depend on the materials used; a simple cutter may cost $20, while a fancy one could run several hundred dollars. In the end, you'll probably have a cutter that eventually ends up sitting, forgotten, in your bottom drawer.

The "Pinhole" Cut

The *pinhole cutter,* or *cigar drill,* is somewhat popular. Of all cutters, this one makes the most minor intrusion on the cigar. Usually, it's a simple device that looks like a cone with a small threaded screw protruding from one end. You place the cone over the head of the cigar, and then turn the screw. A sharp point enters the cigar head, drilling into the body about a half inch. A cigar drill requires you to have a steady hand when inserting it into the cap of the cigar.

Cigar Speak

A **pinhole cutter** and a **cigar drill** are cutters that create a small hole in the head of the cigar to create an airhole through which you draw smoke.

This type of cut leaves the head of your cigar almost entirely intact, and for those smokers (like me) who love the pleasing, rounded feel of the cigar head, this alternative is very tempting. By puncturing the head, you leave the cap virtually intact, minimizing the chances that it will unravel.

A typical cigar drill, which makes a pinhole cut.

There are two drawbacks to this type of cutter. The first is that you have to hold the cigar with one hand, and pull the cone against the head of the cigar using your thumb and forefinger. Then, you have to deftly turn the screw with the fingers of your free hand. This leads to a lot of frustrating fumbling.

The second drawback is that these types of cutters usually make too small an airhole for an adequate draw. If you can't get enough air through the cigar, you'll turn blue instead of contentedly puffing blue smoke. My advice is to avoid this cutter.

The "Puncture" Cut

A relatively recent entry onto the market is a *puncture cutter*, which creates a sufficiently large hole to give you a satisfying draw. This cutter is very simple in concept: It's a very sharp blade rolled into a circle approximately the thickness of a pencil. You simply press the cutter into the middle of the cigar head and lightly twist, applying gentle pressure until the blade is inserted to the stop point—about $1/4$ inch.

Cigar Speak

A **puncture cutter** is a type of cutter that, when inserted into the head of a cigar, removes a plug approximately ¼ inch across, creating a large airhole while still preserving the smooth, rounded head of the cigar.

When you gently twist it out, you remove a small plug of tobacco. I've found that with a sharp blade, this type of cutter gives you a sufficient draw and preserves the rounded edges of your cigar head. The puncture cut is my favorite cut.

A puncture cutter.

Several manufacturers make this type of cutter, and most have blades that can be sharpened or cheaply replaced. One cutter on the market is the .44 Magnum cutter, made from a Remington .44 magnum bullet, which sells for under $15. You can order replacement blades for a few dollars.

The puncture cutter does have drawbacks, but the problems are more related to the cigar itself than the cutter. If the cigar is dry, even the slight pressure the puncture cutter requires will cause the end of the cigar to split. This won't happen with a properly humidified cigar, but being delicate creatures, cigars will sometimes just dry out. I always have an alternative cutter to use in case the cigar has become too dry and I don't want to wait to rehumidify it.

The other "problem" is that this cutter won't work on a cigar that has a pointed cap, such as a pyramid. If you want to do a puncture cut on thinner cigars, look for a puncture cutter such as Davidoff makes, which has three different hole-size options in one cutter. You might become a fan of the puncture cut, but you should also consider the most versatile of all cuts: the straight cut.

The Straight or Guillotine Cut

The *straight,* or *guillotine,* cut is by far the most popular. It's the easiest to make, works on all but the very thickest cigars, and opens up almost the entire end of the cigar to draw. The straight cutter is available from hundreds of different manufacturers—and in a few variations on the theme of a single blade that slices down through the head of the cigar.

Cigar Speak

The **straight** or **guillotine cut** lops off the head of a cigar in a straight, clean line, allowing air to be drawn through the cigar. A straight cut can be made using a cutter with one blade or two blades.

With some exceptions, the guillotine cutter has a large hole that can handle a very thick cigar. A blade slides up and down in a track. You place the head of the cigar in the hole, and press down on the blade to cut the cigar.

A single-bladed "straight" or "guillotine" cutter.

If you have a guillotine cutter with a sharp blade, and you line up the cigar so that the cut runs perpendicular to the cigar and not at an angle, you can hardly go wrong. You'll have plenty of draw, and the cut will be so clean that you won't find yourself spitting out bits of filler or wrapper as you smoke. The goal is to slice off the least amount of the cigar possible in order to open up the end.

Most smokers will slice off about $1/8$ inch of the head, which will remove most of the "flag" or "cap." Some smokers do this because the flag (a loose piece of tobacco applied with natural glue as the finishing touch to the cigar) has a tendency to come off while you smoke. If this happens, just peel off the strand of tobacco that's left and smoke on.

Cigar Speak

The head of a premium cigar is covered by a **flag** of tobacco, which is carefully applied at the end of the cigar-rolling process. If applied properly, the flag is smooth, feels good in your mouth, and helps prevents the wrapper from unraveling.

Some smokers use the guillotine cutter to "shave off" only as little as possible of the head—just enough to expose the filler inside and create draw, but not enough to destroy the flag. This leaves the cigar head slightly rounded—something I enjoy.

If the head of the cigar is very flat, this "shaving" is a real challenge and requires a steady hand to remove just the very end of the cap. With cigars that have a relatively pointed head, making a straight cut is easy and requires a guillotine cutter. You simply clip off approximately $1/8$ to $1/4$ inch—just enough to create a draw.

Two Blades Better Than One?

There are variations to the straight cutter. Several manufacturers, notably Davidoff, offer a *double-bladed cutter*. You insert the cigar into the cutter hole and apply pressure with your thumb and index finger to two separate blades. The theory is that two sharp blades coming from both directions will make a cleaner cut.

A double-bladed guillotine cutter.

The single-blade guillotine enters the top of the head and then pushes the cigar against the other end of the cutter.

If your blade is dull, this final action can lead to the tail end of your cut being ragged. With a sharp blade (preferably one made from hardened English Sheffield steel, which maintains a surgical edge for years), the cut is so clean it's like cutting butter with a hot knife.

A problem with inexpensive double-bladed cutters is that there's "play" in the blades, and instead of lining up perfectly at the end of the cut, they meet in the middle of the cigar head and pinch off the last bit. As insignificant as an imperfectly cut cigar might seem, a lot of veteran smokers despise the sensation of a ragged edge—and I'm one of them. If you want to use a double-bladed guillotine cutter, buy a good one such as Davidoff's, and be prepared to spend $50 to $60.

The Scissors Decision

Another straight-cut option is the *scissors cutter,* which looks like a barber's scissors with two curved blades at the end. The advantage of this cutter is that it opens wide enough to accommodate any size cigar: from the narrowest to the largest ring gauge you'll find. The very finest cutters have very sharp blades, but you should test the cutter's sharpness before plunking down up to $100 for one of these things.

Cigar Speak

A **scissors cutter** looks like a pair of scissors but has special blades for cutting a cigar. It delivers a straight cut.

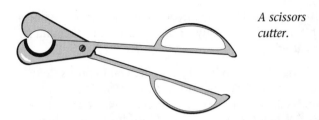

A scissors cutter.

My personal problem with a scissors cutter is that there's no way to steady this cutter, and there's no way to consistently shave off just the cap. If you feel comfortable with the scissors cutter and you find a sharp one, however, it's certainly a reasonable choice.

The Price of a Good Cut

What should you expect to pay for a guillotine cutter? Looks can be very deceptive. A complimentary cutter you get from the tobacconist or the cutter you pay $3 for might serve you in an emergency, but the blades are usually dull and your cut will be rough.

When you're getting started, it's just fine to use one of these, but don't expect more than a few good cuts from a cheap guillotine cutter. The PG (Paul Garmirian) cutter is a very modest-looking guillotine housed in plastic for less than $15, but the guide track is dead-on and the blade is the sharpest steel available. It's short on looks, but delivers hundreds of surgically sharp cuts.

You can also buy very nice cutters, plated in gold, for several hundred dollars. If the blade is razor-sharp and you have the budget, it's a nice extravagance. Remember that part of the enjoyment of a cigar is the ritual, and there is *nothing* like the feel of preparing your cigar with a gorgeous gold- or silver-plated cutter.

However, if the blade is dull, it can't perform the one function it's supposed to perform. Before purchasing any

cutter—especially if you intend to buy an expensive one—
test it out on a cigar. Buy a cigar from your retailer and try
the cutter!

Speaking of razor-sharp edges, I'll let you in on a secret:
I buy a cheap packet of cardboard-encased single-edge
razor blades and drop them in every briefcase and suitcase
I own. When I forget my cutter, I can find one of these
razors, place the cigar on a plate or hold it carefully, and
slice off the tip. It isn't stylish, but it's a darned sharp cut
in an emergency!

C'mon Baby, Light My Fire

You've given your stogie the perfect cut, and you're
ready to fire up. Not so fast! Lighting implements come
in thousands of styles, colors, and shapes, ranging from
the humble paper match to a $2,500 gold and diamond-
encrusted lighter. What you use to light up is a function
of your personal taste (and your budget!), but you need
to remember a couple of basic guidelines when selecting
"fire."

Paper's No Match for Cigars

You don't want your light to contain any chemical flavors
because your cigar will pick them up. For this reason,
avoid paper matches, which have sulfur on the match
head; the sulfur also impregnates the stem of the match to
keep the match burning.

If you're craving a cigar and all you have is a book of paper matches, go ahead, but remember one trick: Don't let
the flame directly touch the cigar. Not only do paper
matches have sulfur in the head to get them started (you
must let this burn off), but they are infused with chemicals to keep the paper burning. From start to finish, they'll
impart a chemical taste if they touch your cigar.

Blowing Smoke

You don't have to let the flame touch your cigar to light it! You can easily light your cigar by holding the flame $1/4$ to $1/2$ inch from the cigar. By drawing in gentle, slow puffs of air, the cigar will heat up and light without direct contact with the match.

You'll probably need several matches to accomplish this no-contact task of lighting up, but it's worth the effort in order to avoid a chemical taste. If at all possible, however, avoid paper matches.

Lighter Fluid Cigar Arson?

For the same reason, I recommend that you avoid any lighter that uses lighter fluid—like a Zippo—as opposed to one that uses a gas like butane. Lighter fluid also burns with a slight chemical taste.

I'd tell you to avoid fluid-fueled lighters, but this is easier said than done! Many interesting, collectible, and attractive lighters are fueled by lighter fluid. Zippo recommends that cigar smokers use the same basic lighting technique that I suggested for paper matches: Keep the flame out of direct contact with the cigar during the lighting process. You then have to decide whether you notice any residual taste.

Wood Is Good

An excellent choice for lighting cigars is the wooden match. Most, but not all, have no chemical additives to enhance burning. To use wooden matches, strike the match and then let the initial flare-up die down.

When the initial flare-up subsides, you'll know that the flame is now feeding on the wood, not the head of the match. To be on the safe side, hold the flame away from the cigar when lighting—just as I suggest for paper matches.

It's a Gas

In the opinion of many aficionados, the butane-fueled lighter is the best. Butane lighters come in a wide range of styles and prices—from 75-cent disposables to expensive and elegant one-of-a-kinds costing thousands of dollars. The easy availability of butane-fueled lighters means there's no excuse for not having and using one. You can find an attractive, refillable lighter for under $20 that will give you years of service.

Technology enables manufacturers to continue developing interesting variations on lighters. You can now buy electronic lighters that use a super-hot coil, rather than flame, to light the cigar. This is a fine alternative to traditional tools, as long as you move the pinpoint dot of heat around the tip of your cigar to ensure full and even lighting.

Another version uses butane to generate something that looks like the flame of a welding torch. This alternative is fine, also, because it uses butane. Use caution and keep the super-hot flame at a slight distance from the end or it could singe the wrapper—or even set it burning at its own pace!

The keys to a good light are generally to avoid lighter fluid, to not let the flame touch the cigar if you have any doubt whether it contains chemicals, and to find something that enhances your aesthetic experience and "lights your fire."

Ashtrays Give Your Cigar a Break

Unless you're a king who flicks his ashes on the floor for others to clean up, you need an ashtray, right? But an ashtray doesn't only contain your ash; if the tray is specifically designed for cigars, it also provides a "resting place" for your cigar.

A cigar needs to be treated gently, and savored. You can't puff too frequently, or the excess oxygen will make the cigar burn fast and hot, releasing bitter tars and oils. Keeping your cigar at a "slow burn" minimizes the heat at the "business end" of the cigar and helps ensure that certain volatile chemicals aren't released. So, you ask, what does this have to do with an ashtray?

An ashtray made for cigars enables you to give your hardworking cigar a much-needed rest as you puff your way to the finish line, and not just any ashtray will do. There are many variations on a theme, but the basic cigar ashtray has a sufficiently long indentation to cradle your cigar and prevent it from tipping into the bowl of the tray or teetering backwards onto the table or floor. A classic cigar ashtray has a "trough" that's several inches long, with a bowl at one end to receive the ash.

Typical ashtrays specially made to cradle cigars.

This tray is functional and elegant—especially in crystal. The only disadvantage of this long trough is that as your cigar becomes shorter with smoking, you're forced to lay the butt of the cigar directly on the glass. Without complete air flow, the head is more likely to remain soggy from whatever saliva remains on it.

To properly support even a very long cigar, you really only need a trough that's an inch or so long. To be sure, a shorter trough doesn't provide quite as much stability at the start of your cigar, but it works better as your smoke progresses because it allows air flow at the head of the cigar.

The Least You Need to Know

➤ Whatever cutter you select, it has to be razor sharp to avoid ruining the tip of your cigar.

➤ *Don't* light your cigar with paper matches or lighters that use fluid.

➤ *Do* light your cigar with wooden matches or a butane-fueled lighter.

➤ Give your cigar a chance to rest by using an ashtray made for cigars.

Chapter 4

Talking the Talk

CIGARS

In This Chapter

➤ Learn how to start talking "cigar speak"

➤ How to read the information on a cigar box

➤ Determine whether your smokes are properly packaged

➤ The difference between handmade and machine-made cigars

You're now able to walk into a cigar shop and start look-ing around. If you're assisted by someone with some cigar expertise who has smoked the cigars on display, you can glean a lot of information. You shouldn't count on find-ing a knowledgeable assistant, however, so it helps to know what to look for and what questions to ask.

Basic Cigar Speak—Talking the Talk

Starting with this chapter, you're going to run into some unfamiliar terms that are used to describe cigars and cigar making. Let's begin with some basic cigar speak—the words you need to know to start having fun with cigars. Later, we'll talk in greater detail about what these terms mean. Here's the "short list" of words you see, along with a clear and easy explanation of each:

➤ **Handmade cigar** When you see a cigar that says "made by hand," you can generally figure that the tobacco leaves were picked, sorted, and bundled by an individual, not a machine. The cigar itself was fashioned by a skilled cigar roller using a few simple tools.

➤ **Machine-made cigar** Most or all of the cigar was made by a machine, and many of the processing stages such as picking the leaves, grinding up the filler tobacco, and rolling the cigar were completed by machine.

➤ **Premium** or **super-premium cigar** This is the cigar you're going to buy because it's made by hand and it's a brand that's consistent from one cigar to the next and from box to box. Because you can't taste-test a cigar before you buy, selecting a premium cigar is one way to improve your odds of getting a great product every time.

➤ **Short filler** The middle of a short-filler cigar is filled with scraps of tobacco, so if you see this phrase on a box, you know it's machine-made.

➤ **Long filler** Long-filler cigars are filled with long leaves of tobacco deftly gathered together by a roller. A long-filler cigar is almost always handmade, and all premium handmade cigars are long-filler cigars.

➤ **Ring gauge** This is a way to measure the thickness of your cigar. Cigar thickness (diameter) is measured in $1/_{64}$-inch increments, so a 32-ring cigar is $32/_{64}$ inch, or one-half inch. A 64-ring cigar (too big to smoke effectively) would be one inch in diameter.

➤ **Length** The length of your cigar is measured in inches or millimeters. I'll use inches in my discussion of cigar lengths, and you can convert to millimeters if you like!

➤ **Shape** For all practical purposes, the shape of a cigar is the length balanced with a particular ring gauge. Some standard combinations of length and ring gauge exist—such as *corona* or *robusto.*

➤ **Color** The only part of your cigar's tobacco that you can see (without cutting it open) is the wrapper. *Color* refers to the shade of the leaf used to wrap your cigar, which can range from light green to almost jet black.

➤ **Strength or body** The relative *strength* or *body* of your cigar, from mild to full-bodied, is one of the most important things to know and also one of the most challenging. You can't tell how "strong" a cigar is by where it was made. Right now, it's enough to know that if you're starting out, start with mild and work your way up.

➤ **Blending** Most cigars are *blended,* which means manufacturers use tobaccos from all over the world to achieve the desired balance of flavor and strength. Like blended whiskey, you never know what tobaccos are used; you have to let your taste be the guide.

The Box Score

Cigar speak is useful when talking to people about various cigars, and also when you're jotting down your personal opinions about a cigar you've just smoked. One of the first places to start is surveying the boxes your cigars are displayed in.

Most of the time, a retailer will display individual cigars for purchase in the original box. Use the information on the box to learn more about the cigar you're considering. Put on your detective cap, and let's check out the clues.

Is It a Premium Smoke?

Brand name is the most obvious clue provided by a box, but there are many other clues. The most critical thing to look for is whether the box is stamped "Handmade" or—in Spanish—*"Hecho a Mano."* A box almost always tells you whether the cigars are handmade.

A box label conveying the romance, brand name, and origin of a fine cigar.

While the stamping "Handmade" is a mark of pride, it doesn't assure quality. It's an art to roll a great cigar, but learning to roll a passable cigar isn't too difficult.

Even if a cigar is handmade, it might have been assembled hastily or carelessly. If you don't see "Handmade" or *"Hecho a Mano,"* you almost certainly don't have a hand-made product. Keep in mind, however, that this is just one of many clues you'll use to find a really good smoke!

Branded a "Winner"

A critical clue in reading a box is who made the cigar. I'm not a slave to labels, but when you're starting out, you have a better chance of finding a good cigar by sticking to the established brands listed in Chapter 1.

Sometimes it's a trick to find premium brands in today's market. Often, the cigars are snapped up by regular customers before they ever make it to the shelf. Take heart: You can find good cigars if you know how and where to look.

The spotty supply of name-brand cigars, as well as the growing number of new cigar retailers who don't have the clout to get them, has spawned a lot of new handmade cigar brands. It's easy to find new cigars, but beware: They may be nothing more than cigars slapped together using tobacco rejected by the big boys.

So many new brand names have cropped up in the past two years that it's almost impossible to keep up. The upside is that you might stumble upon a good cigar that isn't an established brand. After you try some of the major brands, you'll have a benchmark for a good cigar, and you then can experiment with all sorts of new names.

Is Wood Always Good?

Cigars nestled in cedar boxes might seem like a slam-dunk winner. Cedar boxing connotes quality, aging, and craftsmanship. It's true that many of the finest brands—Davidoff, PG, and Avo Uvezian, to name a few—come in cedar boxes. It's also true that many fine brands come in boxes completely covered in paper—A. Fuente, Te Amo, Don Diego, H. Upmann, Partagas, and Macanudo, to name a few.

In cigar speak, cedar is good, but don't assume that a cedar box means a good stogie. The cedar used for making cigar boxes is relatively cheap—too low a grade for use in furniture, guitars, humidors, and whatever else Spanish cedar is used in. A wooden box isn't a guarantee of quality.

Where Was Your Cigar Born?

Most cigar boxes include the cigar's country of origin. Any imported cigar also carries a tax stamp on the box, which tells you where it came from.

So how much attention should you pay to where your cigar came from? With almost all cigars made outside of Cuba, the country of origin means very little these days. This said, some broad generalizations still hold true for many premium cigars. Cigars made in Cuba, Honduras, and Mexico tend to be more full-bodied. Cigars that come from the Dominican Republic and Nicaragua tend to be milder.

Boxed In: Feeling the Pressure

You can also use the box to size up how your cigars have been packed. Two basic types of packing are used: *round pack* and *square pack*. Your basic rule of thumb: Square pack is usually found with less expensive and machine-made cigars, while most premium handmade cigars are round pack. Some cigars, such as the Padron Anniversario series, feature a packing method that renders the cigars almost square—a throwback to the "old days" when many cigars were square-packed.

With square pack, the cigars are essentially pressed into a box so tightly that they conform to the square box. This *box pressure,* as it's called, doesn't make a difference with a short-filler cigar, but it can crush the filler leaves of a handmade cigar and seriously damage its "draw." It can also crush delicate wrappers.

Round-pack cigars are boxed in such way as to preserve the natural round shape of the handmade product. A round cigar is no guarantee of a good smoke or a good draw, but it's a visual sign that you're on the right track.

Cigar Speak

All handmade cigars are round when they're made, and a **round pack** preserves this shape. Certain cigars are pressed so tightly into a box that they assume a slightly square shape from the **box pressure**. If done properly, a square-shaped cigar will taste fine and draw properly.

I've had some very enjoyable cigars that were boxed under pressure and were as square as a nerd at a cocktail party. If you take a pass on square cigars, you'll be missing out on some great ones.

A number of cigar brands, or certain cigars within a line, arrive individually wrapped in cedar or tubed in glass or metal. The cedar wrapping, if it's touching the cigar, may impart an additional pleasant cedar essence, but it won't protect the cigar.

Cigar Speak

You'll sometimes see a cigar or line called 8-9-8. This relates to how the cigars are packed in the box: three layers, with nine cigars in the middle and eight on the top and bottom rows. The box "bellies" out slightly in the middle to accommodate the row of nine. This method is a popular way to box 25 cigars because there's no pressure on the stogies.

Tubes provide no assurance of a quality cigar, but they are a great protection against the rigors of shipping. It's also a great way to transport individual cigars for a few hours while you anticipate a great cigar after a meal.

Don't Let a Machine Make Your Cigar

Don't expect either a great smoke or great tobacco from a machine-made cigar; this product will get you through only until you have the chance to kick back in an easy chair and smoke a true premium product. Machine-made cigars are cheap; if you pay no more than a couple dollars, you'll probably get your money's worth. Machines do a great job of cranking out a consistent product with just the right firmness, no soft spots, and never a hard draw.

"Machine-made" and "short-filler" cigars are almost one and the same, because you generally can't have one without the other! Humans can't sprinkle little shreds of cigar leaf into a cigar shape and roll it. Neither can machines deftly combine and roll long leaves of tobacco into a cylinder that burns evenly. The cigar roller's art is in his hands, and it takes an expert "feel" to use just enough long leaf, compress it just so, and ensure a good draw and even burn.

Hot Tip

Many short-filler cigars are flavored with cherry, anise, rum, and other glycerin-based agents. This might sound like an interesting change of pace, but the flavoring usually exists to cover up really bad tobacco. If you don't want to take my word for it, try a few.

Because handmade cigars are just that—handmade—you'll occasionally find a loser among even the best cigars. They may be rolled too tightly for a good draw, have a spongy spot you might have overlooked, or burn unevenly because the filler wasn't rolled "just so." This is the price of buying a handmade product, but you'll find that with the best brands, such mistakes are rare.

Your initial detective work and knowledge of cigar speak will clue you in to a machine-made cigar. The box will frequently say whether the cigars are machine- or handmade. If, however, the box doesn't specifically read "handmade" or "machine-made," other dead-giveaway phrases to a machine-made cigar are "short-filler" and "contains all natural tobacco product." *All-natural tobacco product* means you're getting some part of the tobacco plant, but you don't know which part.

Sleuthing further, look at the binder of the cigar. Handmade cigars use a binder made from an intact, tough, natural leaf; many machine-made cigars, on the other hand, use a binder made of ground-up tobacco bits that are then processed with a natural "glue" and pressed into long sheets cut to size by—you guessed it—a machine.

Now look at the tip, or head, of the cigar. If the cigar has a plastic tip attached to the head, it's machine-made. No premium handmade cigar has a plastic tip.

Even without a tip, the head of the cigar will clue you in to how the cigar was made. The heads of almost all machine-made cigars are prepunched with a hole. The machines punch the hole and roll the wrapper leaf into the hole to hold everything together. If you clipped such a cigar as you'd clip a long-filler cigar, little shreds of tobacco would dislodge in your mouth the entire time you smoked. I can't think of a handmade cigar with a prepunched head, although a few might exist.

Shorted Out—Turn On to Long Filler

Machine-made, short-filler cigars allow manufacturers to use every scrap of discarded tobacco—including veins and stems, which taste strong and bitter, partially because they have more nicotine than the leaves. Short-filler cigars not only use scraps, but because they are cheap smokes generally enjoyed by stogie-chompers, they frequently use inferior tobacco that didn't make the grade for premium smokes. An exception to the machine-made rule is the Cuban cigar, which we'll discuss in a minute.

With the growing appreciation of quality in everything from single malt scotch to cigars, the short-filler cigar, assembled by machine, would seem to be a dying breed. Most new and younger smokers would rather spend $12 and have one great cigar than use the same $12 for 25 crummy cigars. The times call for moderation—and appreciation of the finer things. Never choose a quantity of machine-made cigars over a few excellent handmade cigars.

While short-filler cigars are in a different league than premium handmade stogies, in a few rare instances a major manufacturer will offer a machine-made short-filler cigar using such exceptional tobacco scraps that you end up with a great everyday cigar at a super cheap price. One is A. Fuente fumas, which are made with the scraps of aged tobacco used in $12 super premium handmades. Another is the F.D. Grave Munniemaker line, which includes some cigars that use all Connecticut leaf (generally used only for wrappers); the leaves deliver an interesting, almost beefy-flavored smoke.

Finally, many smaller Cuban cigars are machine-made with short filler. Whereas a Romeo y Julietta Churchill will be handmade, the petite coronas are made by machine. Many of the smaller-tubed Cuban products are machine-made and are quite a bit cheaper than handmade Cubans. These cigars are one way to enjoy Cuban tobacco on a budget.

The Least You Need to Know

➤ Select handmade cigars, and avoid machine-made cigars.

➤ Use the cigar box to determine the brand, whether the cigar is machine- or handmade, and the country of origin.

➤ Don't make assumptions about whether the cigar is mild or strong based on where it came from.

➤ Buy cigars that have been packed carefully, not squished together.

What You See Is What You Get

You've gleaned as much information as you can by scanning the shelves of cigars, and you're ready to make your choice. And what a selection you have! The most obvious visual characteristics of cigars are the color, the thickness, and the length.

Let's start by figuring out what these important elements mean, and how they combine to create what you see, hold, and puff. Remember, there are three basic parts to your cigar:

➤ **Filler** The tobacco rolled inside your cigar, comprising the bulk of your smoke.

➤ **Binder** The tobacco leaf used to hold the whole affair together in a nice, neat cylinder.

➤ **Wrapper** The smooth, attractive tobacco leaf used to "dress up" your cigar for presentation.

Because you can't see inside a cigar to the binder and filler, the color and appearance of the cigar wrapper is your only visual clue when selecting a cigar. Ranging from green and yellow, through rich orange, tan, brown, and black, the color provides an indication of what to expect in taste.

What's in a Wrapper?

As with red versus white wine, the lighter a wrapper, the milder the taste. A lighter color wrapper will contribute less to the overall flavor of a cigar than a dark wrapper. Although a wrapper accounts for less than 20 percent of a cigar's overall flavor, it's a cigar's most important visual element. Color does not necessarily indicate the kind of tobacco leaf used, and it certainly doesn't indicate whether the cigar is mild or full-bodied.

Hot Tip

Avoid the oft-repeated mistake of assuming that a darker wrapper signals a strong cigar—even if somebody told you so. Although it's true that darker wrappers generally impart a fuller, often slightly sweeter taste, they may be wrapped around a very light, mild binder and filler.

A light wrapper means nothing. Many very full-bodied cigars come with light-colored wrappers. Let's take a look at what you're likely to encounter when you make your selection. Although cigars can fall into at least 50 formal classifications of color, they all are part of six common categories:

➤ Double claro, candela, jade, or American Market Selection (AMS)

➤ Natural or claro

➤ Colorado claro or English Market Selection (EMS)

➤ Colorado

➤ Maduro or Spanish Market Selection (SMS)

➤ Double maduro, oscuro, or maduro maduro

Most cigars with maduro or natural wrappers will be labeled as such, but you'll seldom find packaging that describes the specific wrapper color. This is where you get to be the expert, and make your own decision regarding color. My Descriptive Guide to Cigars (see Chapters 9 through 12) often describes wrapper color, which will let you compare your own evaluation against mine.

Double Claro, Candela, Jade, or American Market Selection (AMS) Wrappers

For years, this was the favorite wrapper of American smokers. It's *flue cured,* which means that after the tobacco leaf is picked in the field, it's artificially heated in barns rather than allowed to naturally cure in the warm breeze. This heating process seals in some of the chlorophyll, which lends the light green hue.

This category fell out of favor because flue curing arrests the natural maturation of the leaf at a very early stage, so candela wrappers are the most flavorless and bland wrappers.

Natural or Claro Wrappers

This wrapper is light brown, and it is the most common color you'll find on premium cigars—both Cuban and non-Cuban. The tobacco leaf used for these wrappers is fully matured and has been allowed to dry naturally and slowly in large, open barns.

The tobacco plants yielding these smooth, flawless natural wrappers have been grown under cheesecloth to protect the color and appearance. Exposure to sunlight tends to darken the leaf. Shade growing, perfectly timed harvesting, and careful air curing results in a silky, tan wrapper.

A claro wrapper has a light, delicate, but distinctively smooth flavor. Like all quality wrappers that have been properly shipped and humidified, it should ideally have an oily sheen, which shows the cigar has been perfectly humidified and that the leaf is exceptional, and a silky appearance.

Good examples of natural wrappers are found on Ashton (renowned for its fine wrappers), Don Diego, and Macanudo. A generally fine example of the Cuban-grown claro wrapper on a Havana cigar is found on the Cohiba, noted for its silky coffee-and-cream texture and appearance.

Colorado Claro or English Market Selection (EMS)

This wrapper is slightly darker than a claro; the Spanish term *colorado* (red) describes the slight dark reddish hue. Some Connecticut leaf falls into this category, depending on the curing process. Most Sumatran and Ecuadorian wrapper leaf would fall into this category, as would the Cameroon leaf. The Cameroon is an exceptionally rare leaf—and one of my favorites.

The Cameroon leaf has tiny bumps and a wonderful oily sheen. As it burns, the ash displays small white bumps against a backdrop of fine gray ash. An aesthetic delight!

You'll find good examples of this wrapper on Dominican-made Partagas cigars and the A. Fuente Hemingway series.

Colorado claro leaf imparts more flavor to the cigar than a natural wrapper; this characteristic is particularly notice-able with the Cameroon wrapper. "Nut-like" and "slightly spiced" are perhaps the closest terms to accurately assess its flavor.

The wrappers on Davidoff cigars are colorado claro at its best. It's a Connecticut shade-grown wrapper, but one of the darkest and richest of this variety you'll find. Other ci-gars featuring a fine colorado claro wrapper include the Dominican-made Montecruz sun-grown and H. Upmann, Honduran-made Hoyo de Monterrey and El Rey del Mundo, and Tampa-made La Gloria Cubana.

Colorado Wrappers

This wrapper is perhaps the connoisseur's delight. This oily, reddish leaf is a joy to behold. This leaf isn't a special variety; it is usually grown in Connecticut, but is also found in varieties grown in the Dominican Republic and Cuba. This is a leaf that the gods of tobacco selected to have exceptional color and flavor—and one that an expert grower knows how to nurture.

The colorado leaf is very aromatic due to its high oil con-tent, and it has a smooth mouth feel. I'm not sure I've seen a satisfying description of the colorado wrapper fla-vor, but I am familiar with the visual and gustatory plea-sures it delivers. You'll frequently find such wrappers on the PG and Avo cigars.

Maduro Wrappers

This wrapper is distinctly dark brown and quite different from the natural and colorado wrappers. The long process used to create a maduro wrapper concentrates the flavor and creates a sweet, pronounced taste—favored by con-noisseurs because of its fullness and richness. The dark color of a maduro wrapper is caused by two factors:

➤ The leaf is left on the tobacco plant for as long as possible before being harvested. After the leaf is picked, it's allowed to air-dry in barns.

➤ The tobacco usually undergoes a process in which it's treated with heat (and sometimes pressure) to draw out the oils and "cook" the tobacco. The oils are then allowed to retreat back into the cigar. This process can be repeated several times, each time making the leaf darker.

A fine maduro leaf should be very dark, oily, and shiny. The process places considerable demand on the leaf, so by nature, maduro leaves must be tougher and thicker. They generally come from a slightly different variety of tobacco, and they are also the lower leaves. Owing to the type of leaf, you can expect small veins and bumps on the wrapper.

The process and leaf combine to create a distinctive, spicy-sweet character—both in the smoking and on your tongue. Few smokers would argue that the maduro leaf lends an exceptional amount of flavor to the cigar—the most of any wrapper. The rich, spicy flavor of a maduro wrapper makes it something best enjoyed by a more seasoned smoker seeking different, fuller flavor.

Fortunately, you can try bolder cigars without moving away from a brand you enjoy: Many cigar makers produce the same cigar with both natural and maduro wrappers. Good examples, albeit challenging to find, are Ashton and Punch Gran Cru maduro-wrapped cigars.

Because of the time required to process the leaf, and also the more limited demand, maduro cigars are generally difficult to find—particularly in today's market, where demand exceeds supply and cigar makers are trying to supply as many stogies as possible to anxious smokers. If you come across a brand you like with a maduro wrapper, consider snapping up as many as your budget will allow. You never know when you'll see them again.

Double Maduro, Oscuro, or Maduro Maduro Wrappers

If it's possible to get darker than maduro, this is the wrapper. Almost jet black in color, it has been subjected to even more extensive processing than maduro wrappers. It imparts a very rich, pronounced, spicy flavor. As with the maduro wrapper, expect a bumpy, somewhat veiny appearance.

Few cigars feature the option of a double maduro wrapper. Punch makes an oscuro-wrapped robusto, and the JR Ultimate cigar offers several shapes with the option of an oscuro wrapper.

Size Does Matter

Ring gauge is the $^1/_{64}$ of an inch question! There are fat cigars and there are thin cigars, and all of them are measured by ring gauge.

You'll hear terms such as "38-ring gauge cigar" (thin) or "50-ring gauge cigar" (fat). After you understand what ring gauge means, you'll be able to easily make a size choice.

Cigar Speak

The thickness, or girth, of a cigar is expressed in 64ths of an inch. This is called the **ring gauge**, which is the thickness if you placed a ring around the cigar. A 64-ring cigar would be an inch in diameter. A 32-ring would be a half inch. Most cigars fall into the range of 38 ring and 50 ring.

Ring gauge is nothing more than a measurement, in $1/_{64}$-inch increments, of a cigar's circumference. (Remember your high school geometry class?) A 64-ring gauge cigar is $^{64}/_{64}$ inch in circumference, or exactly one inch. That's a huge cigar—one you would have trouble fitting into your mouth. A 32-ring cigar is $^{32}/_{64}$ of an inch, or a half inch in circumference—very slim.

Most standard cigars fall between a 32- and 52-ring size. *Ring size* has to do with how much of the cigar's burning tip is exposed to air, and also how comfortable it feels in your mouth. A fatter cigar smokes cooler and slower because more of the filler is exposed to air. Your mouth is only so big, however, and a really fat cigar is tough to get your teeth around!

A lot of what you prefer in a ring gauge depends on what feels comfortable to you, and also how you smoke your cigar. Ring size also has to do with appearance. A dainty woman puffing a 50-ring Churchill will make a statement—but not exactly a dainty one. In contrast, she can sip at the large cigar, which presents a much more lady-like appearance (if that, indeed, is what she's striving for).

By exploring and smoking a variety of stogies, you'll naturally find the ring gauges and lengths that feel best to you.

Eenie, Meenie... Popular Lengths and Shapes

Most brands offer a choice of several popular lengths, and your selection should primarily be your personal preference (or what's available). Various lengths are paired with ring gauges that provide optimal smoking qualities and appearance, and this pairing has led to a group of more-or-less standardized cigar shapes.

Because cigars are such a tradition-filled product, you'll find that most popular sizes have developed standard names. Often, a size was named after a famous smoker who favored it, such as "Rothschild" or "Churchill." Similarly, the shape can dictate the name, such as "Pyramid" or "Torpedo." It's helpful to know the basic shapes and lengths so you can "talk cigar" with your friends, and you'll be better prepared to describe to a retailer the kind of cigar you want.

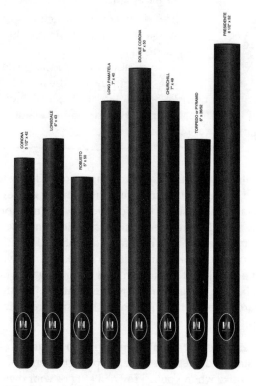

Some of the most common shapes you'll find in the cigar world.

The classic midrange size is the corona, which is generally between five and six inches long and has a ring gauge of about 40. The classic "short and fat" cigar is the

"Rothschild" or "robusto," which averages 4¹/₂ inches in
length and has about a 48-ring gauge. The largest standard
size is the "Churchill," which is approximately 7 to 8
inches long with a ring gauge of 48 to 50.

Cigar Speak

The word **corona**, which is the
mid-sized and most commonly
made cigar, comes from the
Spanish description of the "prime
cut" upper leaves of the tobacco
plant used to make filler. It literally means "fine"
and was originally applied to premium Havana
cigars in a variety of sizes.

The following are the standard shapes you're likely to encounter, along with average lengths and ring gauges. Specific brands will usually employ their own names for these
shapes. I've also provided average smoking time, which
will vary depending on how fast you puff and whether
you're outdoors on a windy day or inside. Armed with
your knowledge of average lengths and ring gauge ranges,
you'll be able to figure out how they match up to the
standard shapes. Starting with the largest, here's the
lineup:

➤ **Gigante, Presidente, Immensa** The largest of the
standard sizes, these are the perfect celebratory
smoke when you're crowned king of your own Caribbean republic! They range from 52 to 64 ring, and
are usually about 8 to 10 inches long. They are almost novelty stogies, but if they're well-made, they
can be a good smoke and a fun gift. A number of
major manufacturers make these available singly,
boxed in cedar. *Average smoke: 1 to 1¹/₂ hours.*

➤ **Double Corona** This smoke hovers somewhere between a 49 to 52 ring and between $7^1/_2$ and 8 inches. These are sometimes misnamed Churchills, which stems from the confusion caused by the different sizes of cigars sent to, and smoked by, the notoriously cheap British prime minister, who could never turn down a freebie. I feel the double corona provides a great balance between length and ring gauge, and it is also a good value because you get almost twice as long a smoke as with a corona, but you generally don't pay twice as much. *Average smoke: 45 minutes to an hour.*

➤ **Churchill** A true Churchill measures approximately seven inches with a 47 or 48 ring. Because of how many makers named products after the famous smoker, however, you'll see Churchills as long as 8 inches and as short as 6 inches. *Average smoke: 45 minutes to an hour.*

Blowing Smoke

Although ring gauge—the cigar's thickness— can dramatically affect a cigar's smoking attributes, length has little influence. A longer cigar will smoke cooler if you're a "hot" smoker and puff too much, but if you allow the cigar to properly rest between puffs, and you're smoking a well-made cigar, any length cigar will smoke cool and pleasant.

➤ **Panatela** These smokes have a ring gauge ranging from 34 to 39, but are approximately 6 to $6^1/_2$ inches long, which cuts a slim, elegant line. The "long panatela" is about a 36 ring but may be up to $7^1/_2$

inches long. The panatela is a relatively hard size to find because a thin, long cigar is extremely difficult to roll, and smokers don't favor them because the burn area is small, which tends to make the cigars smoke hotter than a large ring cigar. *Average smoke: 35 to 45 minutes.*

➤ **Lonsdale** This extremely common and popular size is about 6 to 7 inches long with a standard 42 ring, although each manufacturer will produce variations. The cigar was originally made for the Earl of Lonsdale. Most manufacturers offer a Lonsdale in their assortment of standard sizes, although they'll seldom call it a Lonsdale—usually opting for their own name. *Average smoke: 45 to 50 minutes.*

➤ **Corona Grandes** This cigar is similar to a Lonsdale in length, about 6 to $6^1/2$ inches, but sports a slightly larger ring of about 44 to 46. The corona grandes provides another optimal combination of length and ring gauge. *Average smoke: 45 minutes.*

➤ **Corona Extra, Corona Royale** Yet another variation on the corona, the extra or royale falls somewhere between the classic corona length and the corona grandes— about $5^3/4$ inches with a 44 or 46 ring. *Average smoke: 40 minutes.*

➤ **Corona** The benchmark middle-of-the-road size for all cigar measurement, the classic corona is $5^1/2$ inches long by 42 ring. Most manufacturers offer a corona, but you'll seldom find it called a corona as makers opt for their own romantic or descriptive names. *Average smoke: 30 to 45 minutes.*

➤ **Petite Corona** This cigar usually features the classic 40 to 42 ring of a corona, but is closer to $4^1/2$ to 5 inches long for a shorter smoke. *Average smoke: 25 minutes.*

➤ **Robusto, Rothschild** Originally called a *Rothschild* after the Baron de Rothschild, who favored these stubby wonders, this cigar's classic size is 4¹/₂ inches by 50 ring. You can find variations, of course, but the robusto is distinguished by its wide ring gauge relative to its short length. This has become a very popular size, and for good reason: The wide ring gauge delivers a cool smoke, it doesn't take a major time commitment, and because there's less tobacco, it's an affordable way to sample a brand without taking out a bank loan. Watch out for the Macanudo Rothschild, which may have the Rothschild name, but is actually a Lonsdale. Only Macanudo knows why it named a Lonsdale a Rothschild! *Average smoke: 25 to 40 minutes.*

➤ **Belvedere, Ascot, Demitasse** These are more or less catch-all names for very small, generally thin cigars with rings of 30 to 36 and lengths of 3 to 5 inches. These are not machine-made cigarillos, but actual handmade smokes. Because of the small size, they're tough to make by hand, but a well-made demitasse delivers a short, very satisfying smoke. They have to be savored slowly to avoid overheating! *Average smoke: 15 to 20 minutes.*

Daring to Be Different

Smokes with unusual shapes have certain characteristics that may lend a unique twist to the smoking experience.

➤ **Belicoso, Petite Belicoso** This cigar is noted for its refined, pointed head, which is challenging for the roller to properly fashion. The regular belicoso is about a 48 ring by 6 inches, while the petite version in about a 40 ring by 5 inches. *Average smoke: 30 to 50 minutes.*

➤ **Culebra** This cigar is fascinating and difficult to make and, consequently, hard to find. It's three cigars, each about 34 ring and 5 to 6 inches long, intertwined. To smoke it, you have to unwind the cigars very carefully, and if they're not perfectly humidified, they'll crack. Each cigar will remain somewhat twisted and gnarled, but it's a fun smoke and great to share with two other cigar-smoking friends. It's definitely a novelty, but a nice change of pace. *Average smoke: 30 minutes.*

➤ **Pyramid** This cigar is tough to describe by ring size, because the tip is usually about a 52 ring, graduating down to a pointed 42 ring at the head. Pyramids are usually about 6 to 7 inches long. The idea behind this shape is to give you the largest possible burn area, while giving you a very manageable head. They're extremely difficult to make because the filler leaves have to be deftly rolled to avoid constricting the draw at the head, so this task is usually left to a maker's most experienced rollers. You'll find few pyramids, and even fewer ones with a good draw, but if you do, they're a real treat. *Average smoke: 45 minutes to an hour.*

➤ **Torpedo** This is a peculiar-looking shape, rather than a size. It's tapered at the head, relatively flat at the end, with a bulge in the middle. It got its name because it looks like a torpedo. It's an old-style cigar shape, and was more frequently encountered 100 years ago than today. The torpedo shape is challenging to hand roll, and it doesn't lend any particularly interesting smoking attributes to the cigar, which is probably why you seldom find these cigars. *Average smoke: Varies, depending on the size.*

➤ **Perfecto** A perfecto is another old-time shape, seldom encountered today. It's similar to a torpedo because it has an odd-looking bulge, but unlike the torpedo, it's pointed at both ends. Once one of the most popular shapes, you'll seldom find a perfecto these days. It's usually about the size of a corona, with similar smoking length.

Blowing Smoke

Female smokers have a challenge—a "fatter" cigar gives a cooler smoke, but thinner ring sizes generally suit a woman's face and hand size. Women, if you have the panache to pull off smoking a big cigar, then do it. Buy different sizes, take them home, and decide which one looks and feels best on you.

A cigar's length and shape carries with it certain traditional connotations, which you may or may not care about. Large cigars such as the Churchill, "Presidente," "gigante," or "director" signal bigness, prestige, power, and confidence. A slim cigar such as a "Lancero" or "panatela" is associated with sophistication and elegance. You can also select different shaped and sized cigars to suit the amount of time you have to smoke, as well as how you feel. What kind of mood are you in?

The Least You Need to Know

➤ A smooth, shiny wrapper is your most obvious clue to a good cigar.

➤ Light wrappers don't always mean a mild cigar, and dark wrappers don't always mean a strong cigar.

➤ Thickness is measured by $1/64$ inch, called *ring gauge*.

➤ Ring gauge and length are combined to create standard sizes and shapes.

➤ Choose a size and shape you like.

Chapter 6

It's What's Inside

In This Chapter

➤ Why almost all cigars feature a blend of
  tobaccos from all over the world

➤ How to work your way up from mild to
  "wild," full-bodied smokes

➤ Why you want to try a full-bodied cigar

➤ Determining whether where a cigar is
  made indicates its strength

You've learned about selecting cigars by their color, shape,
size, and packaging—everything on the outside. But a lot
of what gives a particular brand of cigar its unique taste is
what's inside—stuff you can't see, and a blend of tobaccos
you can't figure out from looking at the box! Discovering
what you like is a process of experimenting. Here's a little
broad background to understand better what you're
tasting.

How Your Cigar Is Orchestrated

Most non-Cuban cigars are blended, often using tobaccos from around the world to create a harmonious product. The process is a lot like a symphony orchestra, comprised of the finest international musicians, playing different instruments to create a stirring performance. The manufacturer is the conductor, and in the hands of a relatively few individuals lies the skill to successfully manage this complex process.

Every country, and regions within each country, has unique-tasting tobacco with distinct characteristics. Even the same seed, planted in different countries, will taste very different.

The skilled manufacturer knows how to acquire, test, and compare these tobaccos, blending them in just the right proportions to create a "signature" taste that's consistent year in and year out. Manufacturers reveal very little about the combination of tobaccos used in their cigars. It's enough to know that when you buy one of their brands, you know to expect a very similar tasting product.

Cigars of different sizes, but within the same line, are generally blended to taste the same whether you smoke a chubby robusto or a large double corona. Brands such as A. Fuente and Davidoff have particular sizes that sport unique blends, but this is rare.

Numerous cigar-savvy books and magazines have claimed that cigars of the same brand and line taste different. Most manufacturers would disagree. If you were to compare two different lengths from the same line, you might notice subtle differences, but those differences typically are not because of a blending change by the manufacturer. Although there are exceptions, most manufacturers keep the mix the same throughout lines.

Blowing Smoke

Several manufacturers produce completely separate lines of cigars—with notably different tastes. Look for the full name to guide you. For instance, Punch and Punch Gran Cru are both Punch cigars, but they have very different tastes. Different sizes of cigars within each line, however, generally taste about the same.

I'm giving you a basic rule you can take to the humidor with you: Most brands employ basically the same blend of tobacco, regardless of length. To nail down just the right burn characteristics, the cigar maker may make slight adjustments to a blend based on length, and as you read on, you'll start to understand why the tastes differ. At this point, it's enough to remember that most makers use the same blend in all the different sizes of cigars they make, so the taste will be very similar.

From Mild to Wild: Work Your Way Up

One of the most important jobs a cigar maker has when blending cigars is to give the product a certain "body" or "strength." Many factors influence what makes a finished cigar tobacco mild or strong; we'll explore all these variables later in this chapter.

A full-bodied cigar isn't strong or harsh, but a "heavy" smoke may be a little more challenging for a beginner to appreciate. "Heavy" usually means the leaf has higher tar and nicotine content, and until you learn to appreciate these flavors, you're better off sticking with milder cigars such as Macanudo, Montesino, Baccarat, and others.

Hot Tip

In a nutshell, the major attribute of a "heavy" cigar is a higher tar and nicotine content. While tar and nicotine are detrimental to inhale, they also lend fullness, roundness, and richness to the smoke. These attributes are all positive, which is a good enough reason to puff and savor—but never inhale—a cigar.

When you're shopping for milder smokes, you can really benefit from the guidance of a sales assistant who has tried the various cigars. If you can't get this kind of guidance, your best bet is to experiment!

"Pumping Up" to a Full-Bodied Smoke

A heavier, more full-bodied cigar is sometimes called *Cuban-style* because even though there are some mild Havanas, the traditional Cuban preference has been for a robust cigar. Somewhere on your journey toward the wild side of cigars, you may decide to get off, finding a full-bodied cigar simply doesn't suit your taste. This preference could change as time passes, but listen to your taste buds.

A Saturday morning smoke, for example, may be a perfect opportunity to enjoy a very mild petite corona. As the grand finale of a rich, heavy meal with several wine courses, a full-bodied cigar will send a loud and clear message to your taste buds, whereas they might not even notice a mild cigar.

As you smoke more and richer cigars, your taste becomes acclimated to the higher tar and nicotine content of full-bodied stogies. In my extensive tastings and samplings with those who enjoy spirits such as scotch whisky or brandy, a similar transformation takes place. Beginners opt for light, mild, lower proof spirits; the higher alcohol content and complexity overwhelms their senses. With time and tasting experience, they become used to higher proofs and are also able to identify the subtleties of older spirits.

Like alcohol, tar and nicotine provide the double-edged sword of use and potential abuse. Remember, moderate use and enjoyment may help minimize the health risks that are associated with excessive drinking or smoking.

Is This a Strong Cigar?

Even though you'll hear the term "strong" used to describe a full-bodied or "heavy" cigar, many connoisseurs cringe at the term. To many aficionados, a strong cigar is a harsh, undesirable cigar. "Strong" means that for any number of reasons, the stogie grabs you by the throat and shakes you around a bit. A strong cigar might make even a veteran smoker queasy.

A cigar may be strong, or harsh, because the nicotine and tar content is excessive. It could be that the tobacco isn't of good quality. The biggest failing in cigars, assuming that the basic tobacco is of good quality and it's well made, is that the leaf was improperly or insufficiently cured, processed, and aged.

Young or *green* tobacco—no matter how good the basic leaf is—will make you feel ill if you smoke it before it's fully aged. Green tobacco is not literally green; it's leaf that hasn't had enough fermenting, which is an important process. Green tobacco can make even the most experienced cigar smoker queasy because it's filled with bitter tars, nicotine, and ammonia, which it releases when lit. The cigar tastes bitter and harsh, and the released ammonia makes it stink big time.

Cigar Speak

Tobacco that has been insufficiently cured, processed, and aged is called young or **green** tobacco. Proper processing removes many chemical compounds that make tobacco harsh and strong. Even the best tobaccos, without proper maturation and mellowing, will make you sick. The tobacco maker's art is to convert a green leaf into a rich, mellow cigar.

The nicotine content of young tobacco is exceptionally high, and it contains a great many natural compounds that do not taste pleasant when burned. During the aging process, these either disappear or fall to acceptable levels.

To avoid bad cigars, try the very best cigar you can find as you move up the "relative strength" ladder. You're far more likely to find a properly aged, properly made cigar, which at least lets you make an accurate decision regarding whether you like fuller-bodied smokes.

If you think I'm advocating that you at least *try* to work your way to heavier smokes, you're right. Many, if not most, aficionados end up enjoying heavier cigars; these cigars are the pinnacle that lets you look down and appreciate the various stages of the climb. And just because you enjoy a "heavy" cigar doesn't mean you can't appreciate a variety of smokes.

Finding a Heavenly Body

As cigar making in non-Cuban nations has matured over the past three decades, the country of manufacture means less and less. It used to be that specific countries produced mild or strong cigars. For example, the Dominican Republic once was associated with producing mild cigars, while Honduras was known for rich, full-bodied cigars. Now, some of the world's most full-bodied cigars come from the Dominican Republic, and very mild cigars are made in Honduras.

Not only do these countries have access to tobaccos from all over the world, but makers in these countries have expanded their lines to include a variety of different styles. You'll learn a lot more about the tobaccos associated with particular nations and growing regions in Chapter 8, but don't get hung up on where a cigar is actually made. Yes, this makes your job in selecting cigars a bit tougher, but you'll soon have the knowledge needed to make your selection regardless of where a cigar was born.

If I had to make a broad generalization, I'd say that the best cigar tobacco in the world is coming from the Dominican Republic, and the majority of the finest cigars are being made there. The Dominican Republic has taken the place of Cuba as the world's premier cigar-manufacturing nation.

Strength Is Relative

To help you figure out which brands are mild and which are wild, I've developed a "relative strength guide." It works a bit like a thermometer: Start with the mildest cigars at the top and work your way down to the heartiest, most robust cigars available.

The guide reflects my personal taste, but most experienced cigar smokers would generally agree with my assessment. You can work your way along the scale, experimenting and gradually progressing to the more full-bodied smokes.

I've only listed major, established brands. Many new cigar names are popping up, but few of them have consistent nationwide distribution. I've also found the quality of these newer brands to be spotty because the supply of tobacco is inconsistent. You may not be able to find all of the brands listed in this strength guide, but you're sure to find representative brands in each category.

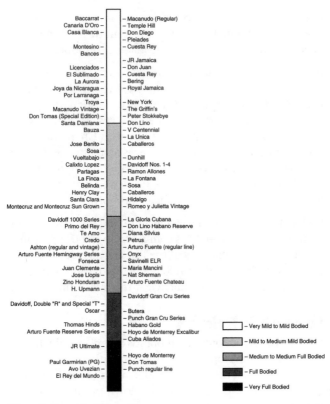

The relative-strength guide.

The Least You Need to Know

➤ Most cigars use a blend of tobaccos from all over the world.

➤ If you're just starting out, try mild smokes.

➤ A cigar that makes you sick may have badly cured tobacco.

➤ Don't assume a cigar is strong because of where it's made.

Chapter 7

Making a Home for Your Cigars

After you start buying more cigars than you can smoke in a week or so, you become a "cigar steward." You are now personally responsible for taking care of your premium smokes and ensuring that when you get around to smoking them, they're as fresh and moist as the day you bought them.

Top Reasons for Stashing Stogies

You can sometimes get a small discount—usually no more than 10 percent—if you buy a box of cigars; volume purchasing isn't a top reason for buying a box. Although saving a little money is a valid consideration in buying a box of cigars, there are better reasons:

➤ If you find a cigar you like and the retailer has a full (or almost full) box, odds are that each one in the box will taste more or less the same.

➤ A brand you like today may taste very different— probably worse—in six months if the maker can't obtain the same quality leaf in the next order.

➤ You have the chance to hedge against price increases, which are now occurring regularly.

➤ Stocking up gives you the chance to age cigars, and while most cigars won't change dramatically, some do benefit from aging and mellowing.

Making a Home for Your Cigars

You'll recall (from Chapter 2) what happens if a cigar seller doesn't maintain proper humidity for the cigars: tinder-dry, crumbly cigars that burn hot and fast. But do you have any hope of replicating the tropics in your own home? Here are the consequences any extreme will have on your cigar stash:

➤ **Too Dry**   If the humidity around your cigars drops below 60 percent, moisture and the volatile oils that pack a lot of the flavor begin to evaporate. The stogie gets dry, brittle, and hard. If you smoke it in this condition, the wrapper will probably unravel and the dry tobacco will burn hot and fast.

➤ **Too Moist**   If the humidity exceeds 80 percent, mold can start to develop. In the early stages, you can wipe off the mold, but if it lingers, it'll take over, and moldy cigars taste like a musty basement smells. Moisture is absorbed faster by the filler tobacco than by the binder or wrapper, so the filler will swell and split your cigar.

➤ **Too Hot** If your cigars are exposed to a heat source, such as a radiator or heating duct, the moisture will evaporate very quickly. Cigars cannot stand long periods of intense heat or sunlight. At best, they'll discolor and quickly give up the oils that contain their flavor. At worst, they'll dry out and split open.

➤ **Too Cold** Cigars can get too cold. Refrigeration or freezing ruins cigars because it removes moisture. Never, *ever* chill your cigars. For the same reason, don't leave them in a car during winter.

Just Right: The 70/70 Rule

The basic rule is to keep your cigars in an environment with 70 percent humidity, at a constant 70° Fahrenheit. This mimics the tropical climate in which your cigars were made. Because you can't measure humidity without an expensive *hygrometer* (a device used to read and measure humidity levels), give your cigars the "pinch test" at least every two weeks.

Cigar Speak

A **hygrometer** is used to read and measure humidity levels. There are a few digital versions, but most look like a meat thermometer, with a needle and markings from 0 to 100 percent humidity.

The bottom line is: You gotta get a humidor! From the day you buy your smokes to the day you light up, humidifying a cigar is a "lifetime" commitment—the life of the cigar! Now, let's talk humidors.

Humidors: From Palaces to Plastic Bags

A humidor maintains a constant balance of moisture around the cigars. Unless you have an expensive, self-regulating walk-in humidor or cigar vault, you'll need to monitor your stored smokes regularly. You'll have to add water to whatever humidifying element you use: Sometimes every few days when the heat's on, or in dry desert climates.

Before we start discussing humidors, let's go over a few cardinal rules to remember when deciding where to store your cigars or locate a humidor:

➤ Never keep cigars anywhere that's prone to mold or fungus. No damp basements! No matter what you use to store your cigars, those mold and fungus spores will find the tobacco because it is a natural vegetable product. (If your basement is cool and dry, then it's a fine place to store cigars.)

➤ Never store cigars in any room that has dramatic swings in temperature. No matter how well you humidify cigars, they won't survive the heat of summer and the chill of winter.

➤ Store your cigars inside, even if you don't smoke inside. Avoid storing cigars in garages or outbuildings; not only is the climate too variable, but cigars will invite bugs and mold. If you have an attached, heated garage, you can probably store your cigars there.

Let's look at some of your options. These selections start at the bottom of the price ladder and work up. With humidors, the most expensive solution isn't the only solution!

Cigar Shop and Cigar Club Lockers

If you don't want to fuss with storing cigars yourself, try locating a cigar club or retailer offering humidified lockers. For an annual fee, you rent a locker and can pick up cigars during store hours.

Cigar lockers are relatively maintenance free, but they do have drawbacks. First, your access is restricted by store hours. Second, most retailers act a little funny if you trot in with cigars you bought somewhere else. If you buy most of your smokes at that store, this isn't a drawback.

Zip-Seal Bags

You'd think that plastic zip-seal bags would be stretching the definition of a humidor, but this is one of my favorite ways to store my smokes. You have to work a bit to maintain humidity in plastic bags. The bag manufacturers claim that their products are airtight, but my "humidifying elements"—pieces of florist foam (yes, the stuff used in flower arranging)—dry out in time, so the bags aren't perfectly sealed.

If you have several bags and don't open them regularly, you should open them for an hour at least once a month to allow some air to circulate around your cigars, and check them for proper humidification. A modest amount of air flow helps inhibit mold and keep your cigars fresh. If you only keep a few cigars, you'll probably open and close the bag regularly to get smokes, so plenty of air will get in.

Hot Tip

The best fluid for humidifying is distilled water or soft water, although I've used regular tap water with success. Tap water contains minerals that will eventually build up and clog your humidifying element. Unless you have a lot of cigars, a quart bottle of distilled water will last a long time.

Buy the best freezer bags, which use heavier plastic. Look for the quart-sized bags, which hold 25 cigars and still leave room for your humidification element.

Plastic Boxes

Sealing plastic containers—the kinds you can buy at most large grocery stores—are very effective for holding in moisture! Rubbermaid and Tupperware are two leading brands, and they only cost a few bucks. You'll also have to purchase a humidifying element—which I'll get to in a few moments.

Like zip-seal bags, these plastic containers don't allow your cigars to "breathe." If you use plastic containers, open them at least once a month to check your cigars for correct moisture and let the cigars breath some fresh air for an hour or so.

If you use a plastic container, buy a new one! If you use one that has held food, you may attract mold and impart food flavors to your stogies. You may also want to wash the new container thoroughly before you use it. You want to remove the plastic smell and make sure there's no residue from manufacturing.

Tabletop Humidors

Not since the heyday of cigars in the early 1900s has such a beautiful array of tabletop humidors been available. There are lacquered boxes of exotic, hand-worked woods; mind-boggling creations that resemble castles and famous buildings (and cost as much); and brightly stained woods with outrageous inlays.

A *tabletop humidor* holds anywhere from 10 to 250 individual cigars. The ideal humidor is lined with Spanish cedar to absorb and release moisture and buffer the outer wood against the moisture changes that could cause the outer liner to swell, shrink, and crack. The outside wood should be thick and tightly joined at the corners to resist cracking as the cedar liner inside expands and contracts.

My test of a good wooden humidor is to raise the lid about three inches and let it drop. If the box is crafted well enough to create a tight seal, a "whoosh" of air will escape and prevent the lid from slamming loudly. For this reason, be cautious about mail-order humidors. You absolutely must test the seal before you buy!

A large, professional-quality hygrometer isn't practical for tabletop humidors. Don't pay attention to the little circular gauges included with tabletop humidors. They run on a cheap spring coil and won't give you an accurate reading. Check your cigars for proper humidity by applying the pinch test (see Chapter 2).

A box with top-notch craftsmanship will cost at least $500. Expect to pay more than $1,000 for a well-crafted humidor with exotic wood or fancy inlay. That's a lot of money, but many humidors make exquisite tabletop decorations, and they'll last forever—possibly something you hand down to future generations.

You can also find tabletop humidors made from clear and smoked Plexiglas. It's tough to create an airtight seal with this material, but a number of high-quality Plexiglas humidors have excellent seals. You need to treat these models as you would the plastic container mentioned earlier in the chapter. If you're not regularly opening and closing the box, open the lid occasionally to let the cigars breathe.

Your best bet would be to find a Plexiglas humidor with a sealing gasket, such as rubber or nylon, and a lock that holds down the lid. The weight of a wood lid is enough to create a seal, but because Plexiglas is lighter than wood, the same isn't true of Plexiglas. Expect to pay $200 to $400 for a high-quality Plexiglas humidor.

Freestanding "Vaults"

I've seen a lot of freestanding cigar vaults and furniture being offered these days. They're electric and some hook into a water source, so they pretty much take care of themselves. I've even see a few handy individuals make a "poor-man's" cigar vault out of an old refrigerator and a passive humidity source such as water-soaked clay bricks. A cigar vault could be a wise investment if you're spending a few thousand dollars over several years.

I've also seen a hybrid between a humidor and an end table, with either a solid wood exterior to hide your cigars, or glass panels to show them off! They seem to work fine, but they're pricey and don't hold that many boxes.

Built-In Humidors

A built-in humidor would go very nicely with the wine cellar in your multimillion-dollar dream home! Having a built-in, cedar-lined, humidity- and temperature-controlled humidor in your home involves a lot of expense—unless you're very handy, at which point it just involves a lot of *work*. But if you start accumulating a significant number of boxes, turning a closet or basement spot or recreation room into a walk-in humidor might be a good idea. A nicely built walk-in will probably cost you at least $7,000 in materials and labor.

The mechanics of a walk-in humidor are pretty simple. You only need shelves that don't rust and walls that won't crumble or mold under the relentless humidity. I've seen people tile closets or panel them with cedar and, bingo! They have a humidor.

Ideally, a walk-in has cedar walls laid against backer board drywall (the same type drywall used as a base for tiled showers). The drywall will help balance moisture fluctuations by absorbing or giving off humidity. Cedar lining is a nice touch, but isn't essential. The door has to seal tightly and should be made of a material that doesn't easily warp.

If you can regularly monitor the room, you only need a drum-type humidifier that you can switch to high, low, or off to control moisture. You can also buy automatic humidity controls. If the room isn't against an outside wall, you probably don't need a heating or cooling source.

When you reach this level of cigar appreciation, look for ideas by going to retail cigar shops with humidors. If you see a design you really like, ask the shopkeeper for the name of the carpenter.

How Do I Keep These Things Moist?

In the old days, the most common humidifying element was an absorbent clay brick for large humidors and display cases, and small clay discs for small humidors. You can still find these, but this special absorbent clay is hard to locate, and dries out faster than some newer materials.

If you're humidifying an area smaller than a walk-in humidor, you'll simply need to use a small piece of porous material. Most tabletop humidors come equipped with some type of humidification element that attaches to the lid. Most of the expensive ones use simple, cheap florist foam, even though they may tell you it's some magical material. Florist foam is that stiff, absorbent stuff in the bottom of flower vases. It works well at holding and gradually releasing moisture.

Blowing Smoke

Whatever type of humidification element you use, never allow it to touch your cigars. If your cigar has direct contact with water, it will grow mold and be ruined.

Built-in humidifying elements are usually attached by a magnet to the lid of your humidor (or in a drawer below, for some larger tabletop models), away from the cigars. These elements are removable so that you can periodically moisten them. Generally, the foam is enclosed in a vented plastic box.

You can moisten the humidifying elements by dunking them in a half-filled sink, but it's best to use a small squeeze bottle filled with distilled water. Just drip water into the element. Manufacturer's instructions tell you how much, but you'll get a feel based on how your cigars are faring. When you're starting out, it doesn't hurt to check your cigars every few days to correct overly dry or moist conditions. If they're too dry, add more moisture than you did the last time!

Keeping cigars moist is an inexact science, and if you use a tight-sealing tabletop humidor, you may sometimes have to open the top to let out moisture. If the cigars feel a bit spongy or contain a light dusting of mold (which can be wiped off and shouldn't harm the cigar), add less moisture to your humidifying element in the future.

If you're creating your own humidification element, nylon sponge works pretty well, but it can get moldy. Florist foam seems to resist mold. You can buy this foam at craft shops and cut it to size with a kitchen knife. Just drop the moistened sponge or florist foam into a small plastic bag, leaving the top of the bag open. Place the smaller humidifying bag into the large zip-seal bag or plastic container holding your stogies. You may even use a low-tech element like this to supplement the humidity in a regular humidor if you discover that the humidor's element is too small to store your smokes properly.

Aging Your Cigars

Some cigars seem to benefit from being set aside. Overall, the biggest beneficiaries of aging are Cuban cigars, which I think get shortchanged on aging and marrying. I've had Havana smokes that transformed from rough and raw to smooth and delicious with about six months of aging.

Some aficionados say that after you buy a cigar, it can go nowhere but downhill. Time does tend to rob a cigar of essential oils, but with proper storage, this won't happen for many years. Experts can't agree on which brands age best, so your best bet is to experiment with your stash as you build your stockpile of stogies.

Hot Tip

Cigars with darker wrappers will benefit more from aging than those with lighter wrappers, and full-bodied cigars are more likely to mellow and intensify in flavor than mild cigars. This has to do with the higher amounts of oil in the darker and more full-bodied cigars.

I suggest that if you buy several cigars of the same brand and you find the first one to be somewhat harsh, stash the others for at least six months. Then try one and see if it's any better. You might find the flavor greatly enhanced—in which case you'll be thankful you didn't dispose of them.

You Can Take It with You

If you travel or want to take a smoke with you to a cigar-friendly bar, club, or restaurant, you may want to invest in a cigar case or even a small traveling humidor.

Cigar Cases

A cigar case is a container for holding anywhere from one to five smokes. Although designed to fit into the pocket of a sport coat or jacket, cigar cases are still pretty bulky. If you're a man, it's best to stash the case in a side pocket. If you're a woman, use your purse.

Cigar cases are generally made of leather and provide individual pockets for cigars. The best cases use thick, stiff leather. Less expensive cases will wrap a layer of leather around a plastic or cardboard frame to stiffen the case; these cases can work nicely. A fancy leather case can cost several hundred dollars, but you can find a decent model for $50 or so. These cases don't humidify your cigars, so I don't recommend using them for longer than a few hours.

Travel Humidors

If you travel, consider investing in a travel humidor. Most travel humidors are boxes, with locking lids to keep moisture inside and padding to hold the cigars in place; they usually hold from one to ten cigars. Most use small sponges, separated from the cigars. You can rehumidify the sponges, so theoretically you could travel with the cigars for weeks. Travel humidors start at about $30 for a single-cigar tube and may cost up to $250, depending on size, use of rare exterior woods, and ornamentation.

Davidoff makes a nifty travel humidor that looks like a cigar case made of wood. These cases come in different lengths and sizes that can hold up to four cigars. They're too bulky to place in a pocket, but they slip nicely into a suitcase, briefcase, or overnight bag, and they do a good job of keeping your cigars humidified and ready.

You can also put a few well-humidified cigars in a zip-seal plastic bag, but you have to pack your smokes very carefully or they'll get crushed. I'd suggest putting the bag inside a cigar box for protection.

This trick only works if you'll be gone just a few days; much longer, and the cigars will start to dry out. In addition, if you're traveling to a very hot, very cold, or very dry destination, the bag won't protect your cigars for more than a day. You can't enclose a sponge in the bag because it could easily flop around and touch the cigars, ruining them.

The Least You Need to Know

➤ You don't have to spend a lot of money to store your cigars and keep them humidified.

➤ Inspect your stored cigars at least once a month to check for proper conditions.

➤ You can "age" cigars, but they probably won't change much in flavor.

➤ You can transport cigars without humidity for a day; if you're going to travel with them, however, you have to keep them humidified.

Chapter 8

Rating Your Smokes

In This Chapter

➤ How cigar scoring works

➤ What to look for when describing a cigar

➤ The truth about cigar ratings

➤ How to conduct a cigar tasting like an expert

A few years ago, nobody rated cigars. Today, everybody has an opinion! In this chapter, I give you the tools you need to organize your thoughts, analyze a cigar, and keep a record. You can compare and contrast with the "authorities," as well as with your friends. Remember, though, that your own opinion is the most important decision maker.

Going by the Numbers

I use ratings all the time, for many different products and services, and I pay attention to them, too. Sometimes a rating will steer me away from something, but only if it includes pertinent details. I need to know why the reviewer did or didn't like something: what was good and what was bad. Like you, I've sometimes agreed with reviews, and sometimes had a completely opposite reaction from the reviewer.

The same holds true for rating cigars. A meaningful rating has to go beyond a number and a one-sentence description, but most cigar ratings in books and magazines stop with this type of incomplete grading. While the reviewers may have detailed reasons for assigning a certain rating to a certain cigar, you're left in the dark when they don't share. Later in this chapter, I'll give you a rating sheet that will help you evaluate cigars like a pro.

Scoring Your Cigars

For years, wines have been rated on a 100-point scale. Specific attributes win x amount of points, from color and clarity in the glass to the length of finish (how long the taste lingers) after swallowing.

This scale has been transferred to cigars, but the factors that contribute to a final score are still pretty fuzzy. I've yet to see anyone explain exactly what attributes are considered when a cigar is rated, and how much of the score various attributes comprise. We're going to change that.

When I worked in smoke shops, I saw a lot of people select cigars based entirely on the final point tally. They started with the top-rated cigars and worked their way down. I guess that system worked for them, but with what you now know about cigars, you'll want a rating and review with a little more substance. You may also want to do your own rating and analysis.

When to Forget a Rating

I don't pay much attention to a rating accompanied only by a brief, fuzzy description of a cigar's flavor. I want to know how the wrapper looked, how even the draw was, how evenly the cigar burned, whether it became bitter or harsh tasting toward the end of the smoke—all that good stuff.

I'd also suggest that you forget the ratings of a cigar you really want to try. Just because a cigar received a bad rating from a so-called expert doesn't mean you won't love it, and vice versa. Ratings and descriptions can help you get started, but the only real measure of whether a cigar is good is whether you enjoy it. It really doesn't matter what anyone else thinks or says.

The role that price should play in rating cigars is another hotly debated issue. Some cigar ratings are weighted for price, and I feel this system is wrong. In some publications, I've seen superior cigars receive lower ratings than lesser smokes because the top smokes were pricey. I'd rather have one great $90 cigar than two good cigars, even if the great cigar is pricey. In the next four chapters, price plays no role in my overall ratings. But I'm happy to tell you if a cigar is both a great smoke and a good deal!

So forget price-weighted ratings, or ratings that don't give you the inside information. Because I haven't seen any ratings that are this thorough, I'm telling you to do your own scoring and judge for yourself! Let's talk about what goes into describing, and then rating, your stogies.

A Funky, Earthy Taste with a Hint of Berries? NOT!

Many cigar ratings use terms like *coffee, nutmeg, cinnamon, straw,* and *leather* to describe cigars. I don't find these flavors in cigars, which defy comparison with any food item. Once in a while, you might sense cinnamon, a nuttiness, or spice, but I have failed in years of tasting to associate various herbs, spices, berries, or nuts with cigar leaf.

The point is, you don't need to fish around for food adjectives to describe your cigar; plenty of relevant phrases are available. Let's take a look at the truly important flavors and characteristics to concentrate on when tasting and scoring a cigar.

What You DO Taste

You experience a cigar with two basic areas: your tongue and your sinuses. Using both, you can detect whether a cigar is peppery or spicy from the "zing" you feel on your tongue and up into your sinus cavities. While your tongue provides very basic readings of taste, your sinuses detect the subtle variations of flavor that are difficult to describe.

How to "Taste" Your Cigar's Aroma

When you smoke a cigar, you detect a lot of subtle flavors as smoke escapes into your sinuses. You can maximize this capability when you taste-test cigars by allowing some of the smoke from your cigar to escape into your sinus passages without inhaling the smoke.

Getting the smoke into your sinus passages takes practice, but you'll know if you have the technique because you'll be able to blow smoke from your nose. I wish I could tell you more about this technique, but it has to be practiced and perfected, not described. Okay, I've talked enough about how to taste cigars. Let's get started.

How to Describe a Cigar

Take a minute to look at the categories I've included in the blank cigar rating sheet. Feel free to copy this sheet, or the one in the front of this book. (Even the publisher says it's okay!)

CIGAR RATING SHEET

Cigar Brand_____   Size Name_____

Length/Ring Gauge_____   Purchase Date_____

Box or Individual_____   Smoking Date_____

Cigar Band	Packaging_____
	Price (Per Cigar or Box)_____
	Where Purchased _____
	_____

Meal/Beverage _____

Overall Appearance and Presentation of Cigar_____Points (Max. 20) **Grade**_____

Wrapper Color_____   Consistent Color within Box?_____

Oily/Dry?_____   Veiny/Smooth?_____

Cap Construction_____   Packaging_____

Ease of Cutting _____   Construction (soft, hard?)_____

Lighting and Burning Properties_____Points (Max. 15) **Grade**_____

Even Initial Light?_____   Even Burn? Initial?_____50%?_____75%?_____

Ash (solid and white/black and crumbly?)_____   Burn rate (fast, perfect, slow?)_____

Resting Smoke (light and even/smouldering?)_____   Require Re-Lighting?_____

Construction_____Points (Max. 30) **Grade**_____

Initial Draw?_____50%?_____75%?_____   Wrapper Stays Intact?_____

Taste_____Points (Max. 35) **Grade**_____

Light, Medium, Full-Bodied?_____   Bitter/Harsh/Smooth?_____

Sweet/Salty?_____   Bland/Vegetal/Spicy/Peppery?_____

Describe Any Changes in Body or Flavor_____

_____

Aroma (rich and smooth/strong and acrid?)_____   Finish_____

Comments_____

_____

_____

Total Score/Grade_____

I've designed my rating form to take you step-by-step through the entire process. I start with where and when you bought the cigar and take you to the finish, or aftertaste, when you set the stub in your ashtray.

Hot Tip

The aftertaste of a *good* cigar will dissipate quickly. The smell won't linger in your curtains or furniture, either. Improperly fermented tobacco contains traces of ammonia, which cause most of the stench in a bad cigar. A good way to test the cigar is to smoke it in a well-ventilated room and see whether the smell virtually disappears within two hours.

You'll notice that the rating sheet contains four main categories, each with a maximum number of points that add up to 100. I use a 100-point scale because it's the most common, and I also provide a letter grade in case you want to see how smart your cigar is!

The four main categories are:

➤ Overall Appearance and Presentation of Cigar (20 points maximum).

➤ Lighting and Burning Properties (15 points maximum).

➤ Construction (30 points maximum).

➤ Taste (35 points maximum).

The categories and the importance I give them is my opinion. If you have a different grading scale, feel free to change the points, as long as the maximum score of the categories adds up to 100.

Prime Factors

Some factors are so important to the enjoyment of a cigar that they overwhelm everything else when it comes to rating that cigar. These factors appear in different categories on the rating sheet. And here they are:

➤ A proper *draw*, which ensures you can get proper smoke volume out of the cigar without working too hard.

➤ Properly fermented and aged tobaccos, which means you won't get sick smoking the darned thing.

➤ An even *burn rate*, which means you won't be watching one side of your cigar virtually burning up while the other side lags behind and smolders.

If any of these factors aren't present, the cigar is worthless. Deficiencies in any of these areas should knock a lot of points off your rating. That's why my cigar rating sheet puts an emphasis on these factors.

Appearance

You know that visual appeal is important, and you know what it can tell you about a cigar. It's your first clue as to what to expect when you smoke the cigar. The various aspects of appearance are worth 20 points maximum. The subcategories I've included are pretty self-explanatory, so let's move on.

Lighting and Burning

A stogie's capability to burn evenly indicates that it's well-constructed. Uneven burning is a nuisance to deal with. A cigar that burns too fast (usually because it's rolled too loosely) means the tobacco will combust at too high a temperature, releasing bitter-tasting chemicals and tar. A cigar that burns too slowly (usually because it's rolled too tightly) will force you to puff harder, overheating the to-bacco. A slow-burning cigar is also more likely to go out or smolder. This important category is worth a maximum of 15 points.

Construction

This small and simple category carries a lot of weight, with a maximum 30-point score. Obviously, I put a lot of emphasis on construction. A cigar that's too loosely filled will burn too hot and, although it's still smokeable, it'll get a low grade from me.

A cigar with little or no draw rates a big, fat zero in this category. Construction and burning are allied, because a badly constructed cigar will probably burn unevenly. However, they can differ; a cigar with a relatively even burn, for example, can be too tightly rolled to draw properly.

Taste

This is by far the most subjective category, but also the most important. Here, you get the chance to decide for yourself whether you think the cigar has a taste that appeals to you. There are some specific things to look for, particularly whether you can smoke the entire cigar without it turning bitter.

As they burn down, a lot of cigars have a tar buildup that makes them turn harsh and bitter. In fact, so many cigars do this that a lot of smokers expect to abandon their cigars anywhere from half to three-quarters through the smoke. Don't accept this from a cigar. I've smoked many cigars to the nub, so I know that a really great stogie will give you a pleasurable smoke until it burns your fingers. If I have to toss a cigar before it's at least 90 percent gone because it gets bitter or harsh tasting, that cigar deserves a major point deduction.

Finally, I don't assign specific numbers to each subcategory, such as the appearance of the ash or the burn rate. You can break down your rating if you like, assigning as many points as you wish to each subcategory as long as they add up to the total for each of the four primary categories.

"Dear Diary..."

Each time you try a new cigar, or revisit a brand, take a few moments to fill out a rating sheet and compile a diary, or log, of your adventures. If you sample enough cigars, you may start to forget what you thought of a particular smoke. This way, you have a permanent record to which you can refer. You can compare your own tastings at a later date, and also compare it to others' opinions.

The best way to learn how to rate smokes is to see how someone else rates them. This section walks you through how I rated a cigar, and how I used my rating sheet to describe the experience (see page 104).

To make my tasting as close as possible to the experience you might have, I picked a cigar I had never smoked before: the Fuente Fuente OpusX. This cigar is a hard-to-find, relatively new offering from a fine manufacturer.

To let you see more easily how I achieved scores for each category, I've put my individual subcategory scores in brackets. It's your option whether or not you want to use subcategories or just give an overall score.

Here goes.

Appearance and Presentation

First, I jotted down everything related to buying the cigar: size, shape, length, ring gauge, and where and when I bought it. When I purchased the cigar, I compared it to the others in the box and they were identical: all similarly colored and all firmly and evenly constructed. In the cedar box, the large and colorful bands and perfectly matched wrapper leaves made a very nice presentation.

I examined the wrapper: a lovely, deep, reddish-brown colorado. Fuente is growing this wrapper leaf in the Dominican Republic, and it's being hailed as one of the most successful efforts so far to grow fine wrappers in that country. In appearance, this is as fine a wrapper as you'll find.

The construction of the cigar seemed flawless, which is typical of Fuente. The cap was seamlessly applied, and the wrapper had a light oily sheen, but was more toward the dry side. I like to see more oil, but it doesn't really matter as long as the wrapper is supple and has some "give" when squeezed.

CIGAR RATING SHEET

Cigar Brand __Fuente Fuente OpusX__   Size Name __Robusto__

Length/Ring Gauge __5 by 50 ring__   Purchase Date __April 22, 1997__

Box or Individual __Individual__   Smoking Date __May 4, 1997__

Packaging __Boite Nature/cello wrap__

Price (Per Cigar or Box) __US $12.50__

Where Purchased __CPCC International Cigar and Pipe Exposition__

Meal/Beverage __After light meal; smoked with Ferrand XO Cognac__

Overall Appearance and Presentation of Cigar ___20___ Points (Max. 20)   Grade ___A+___

Wrapper Color __Colorado (4/4)__   Consistent Color within Box? __Yes (2/2)__

Oily/Dry __Light Sheen (2/2)__   Veiny/Smooth? __Flawless (5/5)__

Cap Construction __Excellent (1/1)__   Packaging __Very Good (2/2)__

Ease of Cutting __Perfect (2/2)__   Construction (soft, hard?) __Firm -- Slightly hard (2/2)__

Lighting and Burning Properties __15__ Points (Max.15)   Grade __A__

Even Initial Light? __Yes (1/1)__   Even Burn? Initial? __Good__ 50%? __OK__ 75%? __Good (12/12)__

Ash (solid and white/black and crumbly? __Firm; lt. gray__ Burn rate (fast, perfect, slow)? __Slow but OK (1/1)__

Resting Smoke (Light and even/smoldering)? __Light/even (1/1)__   Require Re-Lighting? __No (1/1)__

Construction __26__ Points (Max. 30)   Grade __A-__

Initial Draw? __Good__   50%? __Tight__   75%? __Good (24/27)__

Wrapper Stays Intact? __Split Slightly at end (2/3)__

Taste __35__ Points (Max.35)   Grade __A+__

Light, Medium, Full-Bodied? __Full-Robust__   Bitter/Harsh/Smooth? __Smooth__

Sweet/Salty? __N/A__   Bland/Vegetal/Spicy/Peppery? __Spice/cedar hints__

Describe Any Changes In Body or Flavor
__Started medium body and built to more robust at 2 inches__

Aroma (rich and smooth/Strong and acrid) __Rich__   Finish __Pleasant__

Comments
__Smooth & rich; superior aged leaf throughout; overly firm draw midway diminished smoke volume slightly; large band was tough to remove. Fine smoke. Powerful, complex flavor.__

Total Score/Grade   __96/100__   A

When I squeezed the cigar, it seemed a bit firmer than I like, but the others in the box were equally firm. There were no spongy spots, but I did have a slight concern about whether the cigar might be too tightly rolled. My judgment call was that it felt fine.

Typical of Fuente, each cigar was encased in a cellophane wrapper. I noted (although I didn't see a need to jot it down) that the cellophane slipped off easily. Had it been too tightly applied to the cigar, as some cello sleeves are (I've never had this problem with a Fuente), I might have had to tug it off and risk tearing the wrapper leaf. Should this have happened, I would have noted it in the comment section.

So, with the exception of the slightly firm construction of the smoke, the appearance and presentation was perfect. Some smokers might take a point off for the cellophane wrappers, because they don't look as stunning in the box as unwrapped cigars. I don't. I gave appearance and presentation 20 out of 20 points, or a solid "A."

Before I began to smoke, I noted when I was smoking it, and what meal came before it. In this case, I had a light stir-fry meal, cleared my palate with some water, and settled down with one of my favorite cognacs. Of course, if you aren't sitting around with pen and rating sheet in hand, you can write notes later from memory. It's best, however, to rate immediately, while the experience is fresh.

Lighting and Burning Properties

Time to fire up! A critical part of enjoying a cigar is how well the cigar burns. As we've discussed, a cigar that doesn't burn evenly is frustrating to smoke. It may also be a sign of poor bunching of the filler tobaccos and uneven aging of the leaf. So in my guide, burning characteristics are worth 15 percent of the total score.

I examine how quickly and evenly the cigar lights when I char the tip, or foot, with my flame. (I'm assuming, of course, that your cigar has been properly humidified before you smoke it. If the stogie's too dry or too moist because you haven't given it the right climate, you can't fault the cigar.) The Fuente Fuente OpusX lit perfectly and evenly.

If you don't have a companion to help you judge aroma, this is the best time to judge for yourself. As the tip begins to give off smoke, use your hand to fan a bit of the smoke to your nose; your ability to really smell a cigar becomes blunted once you start smoking. Why? Beats me, but it's true.

The rating sheet leaves room for you to grade how even the burn is in the beginning, halfway through, and near the end of your smoking experience. A cigar can start off uneven but settle down into a nice even ring after an inch or so. The cigar can also begin evenly, and then start to degrade.

Ideally, the burn should be perfect at all stages. My Fuente Fuente OpusX started off perfect and even, leaving a firm, light gray ash (also noted). This cigar ash easily reached almost an inch before needing to be gently tapped off the cigar.

Midway through the cigar, the tip began to burn somewhat unevenly, but it wasn't a problem. The cigar then settled back into a perfect and even burn all the way to the end. No points deducted for its burn.

As it rested in the ashtray, the cigar gave off a very light plume of gray smoke. If it had been too loosely rolled, or the filler had been unevenly bunched, it might have smoldered or burned too quickly. The lighting characteristics and burn rate were ideal, so I gave it 15 out of 15 points or an "A" grade.

Construction

This category has few variables, but it carries a lot of weight in my rating. It was here that the Fuente Fuente OpusX showed its only weakness.

The cigar started with a nice draw. The draw became a little too tight halfway through the cigar; perhaps as the tobacco heated up, the filler expanded a bit. This slightly difficult draw, which wasn't enough of a problem to lower my score significantly, was the cigar's only flaw, and I noted it in my comments. The firm draw led me to give the cigar 26 out of a maximum 30 points, or an "A+" grade.

Taste

This category has the heaviest weighting, accounting for 35 percent of the total score, but it also contains some of the most complex and difficult to describe stogie attributes. This category is also very personal because it deals with your *opinion* of how the cigar tastes. I can smoke a cigar I hate, but I can give it a top rating for construction and appearance if it meets my criteria. I will, however, downgrade such a cigar based on taste.

How do I grade for taste? Generally, I jot down a few notes about taste while I smoke, and add different notes as I taste different things. I like to wait until a cigar is nearly finished before jotting down my final comments about taste, because a cigar's characteristics can change as you smoke. I do include some basic descriptions in this section that might help guide you. If you like, you might use one rating sheet as a "scratch" copy, and then transpose your final comments to a fresh sheet and to put into your cigar-tasting diary.

The Fuente Fuente OpusX was full-bodied, which is no surprise because the Fuentes like to blend heavier-tasting cigars in the Cuban style. Even though the cigar was "heavy," it was very smooth. This taste reflects the thorough fermenting and several-year aging process the tobaccos used in the Fuente Fuente OpusX receive, and I made an appropriate note in the comments section.

From the first puff to the final stub, the cigar had no trace of harshness or bitterness that would point to insufficient fermentation or aging. Saltiness or sweetness wasn't an issue. Likewise, there was no buildup of dark, bitter tar at the head of the cigar as it neared the finish line—another sign that the tobaccos were perfectly aged.

The cigar was spicy with a bit of pepper, characteristic of the Cuban style. There was no vegetal quality, once again pointing to superior tobaccos that had been sufficiently aged. The cigar did have a hint of cedar, typical of Fuente cigars because they're well-aged in cedar-lined rooms.

I did notice that the cigar started off a bit mild, and then built intensity and increased in body after an inch or so. This characteristic is great in a robusto, which ideally eases you into the smoke and then delivers a lot of flavor in a relatively short time. The change in intensity probably indicates that a slightly lighter filler blend was placed at the foot of the cigar, and heavier tobaccos were used in the remainder of the filler.

As I lay the half-inch stub in the ashtray, my mouth had only the slightest taste of cigar. A bad cigar will leave a sour and bitter aftertaste for up to an hour. The aftertaste of this cigar disappeared quickly. My judgment call was that the taste rated 35 out of a possible 35 points, or yet another "A+."

Comments and Final Scoring

Other than the construction, the Fuente Fuente OpusX was nearly perfect. I loved the luxurious band, but it was glued very firmly and did not readily peel off even as the ash neared the band and warmed the glue. I had to pick off the band carefully, which was a nuisance—but not enough of a nuisance to affect the score.

A bit of excess glue from the band had oozed onto on the wrapper, creating a very slight tear. Because it had no effect on the smoke, I didn't downgrade for this, but it was a close call. Usually, if I'm having real problems removing a cigar band, I'll leave it on until the very end of the smoke. In this case, the band was so large that I had to remove it to finish the cigar.

The four categories added up to a final score of 96, which is outstanding. I added up the letter grades from each category and gave them a loose weighting, earning the cigar experience an "A."

I never like to rate a brand or line of cigars based on just one cigar, and this Fuente Fuente OpusX provides a perfect example of why. I know the quality and consistency of Fuente cigars is very high, and all cigars are carefully inspected and hand-selected. After this first experience with the Fuente Fuente OpusX, I smoked others of the same line and found the construction to be perfect. You'll notice that in my descriptive guide (in Appendix A), I upgraded my score for the line to a 98.

The same make, type, and year of wine doesn't vary from bottle to bottle because it all comes from the same batch of grapes. The only exception is a very old bottle of wine, which may have improved with age, or turned musty or sour compared with another bottle sampled years earlier.

Blowing Smoke

Even the best makers occasionally turn out a cigar that's not quite perfect—that's the nature of a handmade product. Rate several cigars from one line before making your final conclusions about a brand.

Each cigar, however, is unique. If you dislike a cigar and try another and it displays the same negative qualities, don't smoke any more of them. If the cigar you first sample has a few flaws but you like it, keep taste testing.

The Least You Need to Know

➤ The cigars of most brands taste the same and feature the same construction, regardless of size.

➤ Over time, rate several cigars from the same manufacturer so that you can draw more accurate final conclusions about the quality and consistency of a particular brand.

➤ To build your expertise and knowledge of cigars, keep a diary of the cigars you've smoked and rated.

➤ A "blind tasting" is the most accurate way to rate cigars, but you'll need a least one other person to help you conduct one.

Chapter 9

Modestly Priced Cigars

In the next four chapters, you'll find brief descriptions of the strength and attributes of nearly 100 non-Cuban brand cigars. New brands are being added every month, but I've done my best to cover all the established brands, and the newcomers I think stand a chance. I rate entire lines of cigars, not just single cigars or one size. I haven't scored or described a line unless I've had the chance to sample several sizes in order to check for brand consistency.

Here's the key to the information you'll find in each listing:

➤ **Country of origin** follows each brand name. I include no Cuban brands because it's impossible to rate lines that are as inconsistent as the Havanas have become. Because most manufacturers outside Cuba use blends of tobacco from many countries, I don't put as much weight on the country of origin as in the overall strength rating. Countries are abbreviated as follows:

COS—Costa Rica
DOM—Dominican Republic
HON—Honduras

JAM—Jamaica
MEX—Mexico
NIC—Nicaragua
PAN—Panama
USA—United States

➤ **Strength** rating helps you identify the relative strength of the brand.

➤ **Scores and grades** give you two different ways to see how I judged a brand of cigars, and I use the same categories as my rating guide in Chapter 8. I'm not afraid to use the full spectrum of scoring, so a superb line of cigars can earn a near-perfect 98 or "A+," while other lines may get a "D" or 70. You'll find that my good ratings, particularly in the 90s, are higher than you'll see in some other publications, but I think a great brand deserves a near-perfect score.

➤ **Descriptions** include a discussion of notable positives and negatives, as well as basic categories (**Appearance, Lighting & Burning, Construction, Taste**). I've based my ratings and grades on the same rating sheet you'll find in Chapter 8, but for the sake of space, I've provided only a brief summary of each cigar brand's flaws and strengths. "Taste" is more heavily weighted in my grading, so a low mark for taste will pull down the overall grade considerably.

I don't break out individual sizes within a brand, unless I know a particular size incorporates a different blend. Different-sized cigars within the same line usually feature the same blend of filler tobaccos and the same overall characteristics of quality and construction. If a maker has two or more distinctive lines, such as Macanudo and Macanudo Vintage, I differentiate them for you.

Overall, my comments focus on the flaws more than the excellences for the simple reason that I assume a premium, handmade smoke is excellent in all areas unless it proves otherwise!

➤ *Best Buy* means that the cigar combines quality, taste, consistency, and price.

➤ *Great Smoke* means that the cigar is one of my personal selections for a top cigar, regardless of price.

The cigars are divided into chapters by price, like so:

Modestly priced ($3–$6/cigar)
Medium priced ($5–$8/cigar)
Pricey ($6.50–$12/cigar)
Trés Pricey ($8–$25/cigar)

Price within a particular line of cigars is influenced by size: In general, cigars will be consistently priced from the largest to the smallest. As a general rule of thumb, there is no such thing as a particular size that represents a particular value. I like to imagine, cheapskate that I am, that I get the most "smoke time" for my money with double coronas and Churchills, but I have no real evidence to back up that conclusion!

In this chapter, you'll find cigars for the modest budget, then in the next three, you'll gradually scale the heights of cigar connoisseurship. But before you spend $25 on a cigar with a great pedigree but so-so taste, turn to Appendix A to see all the *Best Buys* and *Great Smokes* listed—as well as those that are both a great buy *and* a great smoke!

Bances (HON/USA)
Strength: Mild
Appearance: 14/20 (C+)
Lighting & Burning: 13/15 (A-)
Construction: 26/30 (B)
Taste: 26/35 (C-)
Final Grade: 79/100 (B)

Bances tends to lack any complexity in flavor, but it's a relatively well-constructed brand with good consistency. The tobacco usually shows moderate lack of aging. It's inexpensive for a handmade stogie, but bland.

Bauza (DOM)
Strength: Medium
Appearance: 14/20 (C+)
Lighting & Burning: 13/15 (A-)
Construction: 26/30 (C+)
Taste: 28/35 (D)
Final Grade: 79/100 (B-)

Although made by Fuente, this is a half-step above a bundled cigar and not much attention seems to be lavished on it. Construction is spotty and the cigars sometimes burn unevenly. It lacks any distinguishing flavor. Wrappers are dull and papery.

Jose Benito (DOM)
Strength: Mild
Appearance: 15/20 (B-)
Lighting & Burning: 13/15 (A-)
Construction: 23/30 (C-)
Taste: 25/35 (D)
Final Grade: 76/100 (C+)

Pleasant and undistinguished, with inconsistent and dry wrappers, the tobacco shows signs of insufficient quality and aging.

Bering (HON)
Strength: Mild
Appearance: 15/20 (B-)
Lighting & Burning: 14/15 (A)
Construction: 25/30 (B-)
Taste: 26/35 (C-)
Final Grade: 80/100 (B-)

A few years ago, the maker introduced a handmade version of this formerly all machine-made line. It's a nice, mild smoke, but the flavor lacks much complexity. The wrappers are attractive but dry, the filler tobacco is nice and generally well-aged, and construction is consistently good.

Las Cabrillas (HON)
Strength: Medium
Appearance: 16/20 (B)
Lighting & Burning: 12/15 (B+)
Construction: 20/30 (D)
Taste: 20/35 (D)
Final Grade: 68/100 (C-)

This cigar suffers from inconsistent construction and shows consistently underage tobacco that gives it a vegetal and sometimes bitter character.

Calixto Lopez (Philippines)
Strength: Medium-mild
Appearance: 14/20 (C+)
Lighting & Burning: 13/15 (A-)
Construction: 17/30 (D)
Taste: 20/35 (D)
Final Grade: 64/100 (D)

This is an inexpensive cigar, with a taste to match. The wrappers are dry and papery, and the tobaccos are harsh.

Canaria D'Oro (DOM)
Strength: Mild
Appearance: 16/20 (B)
Lighting & Burning: 14/15 (A)
Construction: 25/30 (B-)
Taste: 31/35 (B)
Final Grade: 86/100 (B+)

Among mild cigars, this is one of the nicer selections. It also benefits from aging at least six months, and will develop additional flavor in your humidor. I have some that are three or four years old, and I'd swear they're better for the aging. Crammed into boxes, the cigars show a lot of box pressure (square instead of round), which is a flaw. Many smokers say the cigar is bland. However, it is an older, established brand and has proven itself over the years with consistent flavor and quality. It combines good taste with a low price. *Best Buy & Great Smoke*

Cuesta Rey (DOM)
Strength: Mild
Appearance: 18/20 (A-)
Lighting & Burning: 13/15 (A-)
Construction: 27/30 (B+)
Taste: 31/35 (B)
Final Grade: 89/100 (A-)

This is a very pleasant line made for M&N Cigar by A. Fuente y Cia. It's well made, extremely consistent, and available with natural or maduro wrappers that are generally a bit on the dry side. It is a good but not a great or complex smoke. For the money, however, it's an excellent value. *Best Buy*

El Rey del Mundo (HON)
Strength: Medium to heavy
Appearance: 18/20 (A-)
Lighting & Burning: 13/15 (A-)
Construction: 24/30 (C+)
Taste: 22/35 (D)
Final Grade: 77/100 (C+)

To my taste buds, the El Rey is a harsh and heavy cigar. Because I've seen it described as everything from mild to heavy, somebody has to be wrong. You'd better try it for yourself. The El Rey has a peppery, biting taste that some smokers crave. Construction and quality is inconsistent. If you smoke enough of them, you'll find that some are good, but many are not. It's a classic old-style Honduran cigar with harsh tobacco—which I don't like.

La Finca (NIC)
Strength: Medium
Appearance: 14/20 (C+)
Lighting & Burning: 12/15 (B+)
Construction: 23/30 (C)
Taste: 20/35 (D-)
Final Grade: 69/100 (C-)

Like many Nicaraguan cigars that use a considerable amount of Nicaraguan tobacco, occasional cigars in this line can be good, but the quality from cigar to cigar is highly inconsistent. Nicaraguan tobacco crops haven't recovered from that country's civil war, and even when good leaf is produced, it's often skimmed off by top makers in Honduras and the Dominican Republic.

Flor de Florez (DOM)
Strength: Medium
Appearance: 17/20 (B+)
Lighting & Burning: 13/15 (A-)
Construction: 24/30 (C+)
Taste: 24/35 (C-)
Final Grade: 78/100 (B-)

This is an attractively wrapped line of cigars with a middle-of-the-road flavor and decent construction. It's pleasant, not too expensive, and a nice, average cigar.

Arturo Fuente Regular Line (DOM)
Strength: Medium
Appearance: 18/20 (A-)
Lighting & Burning: 12/15 (B+)
Construction: 27/30 (B+)
Taste: 31/35 (B)
Final Grade: 88/100 (A-)

This is a solid brand with lots of sizes and shapes, excellent construction, and good value. In its price range, this is one of the most reliable, consistent cigars you'll find. The cigars are blended to have some spice, and some smokers find them a bit harsh. Box to box, however, you'll get the same consistent taste over and over because Fuente controls much of its tobacco crop, and then blends in leaf from other nations. The company also properly ages its tobaccos. *Best Buy*

Henry Clay (DOM)
Strength: Medium
Appearance: 13/20 (C)
Lighting & Burning: 13/15 (A-)
Construction: 23/30 (C)
Taste: 22/35 (D)
Final Grade: 71/100 (C)

Some folks really like this cigar, and it's easy to find. It has a gnarled, dark wrapper and I find it gets bitter. It's inexpensive, but in this league, I much prefer the Munniemaker machine-made tubed cigar, which uses all Connecticut tobacco and is just as dark and ugly as the Henry Clay, but smoother. Box pressure makes the cigars square.

Hoyo de Monterrey (HON)
Strength: Full
Appearance: 16/20 (B)
Lighting & Burning: 14/15 (A)
Construction: 26/30 (B)
Taste: 27/35 (C+)
Final Grade: 83/100 (B)

This regular Hoyo line is somewhat harsh and overly peppery, consistent with-old style Hondurans. If you like strong Honduran smokes *à la* Don Tomas and Punch, the Hoyo is the best of that bunch.

Montecruz (See Dunhill Montecruz)

Montesino (DOM)
Strength: Mild
Appearance: 17/20 (B+)
Lighting & Burning: 12/15 (B+)
Construction: 26/30 (B)
Taste: 31/35 (B)
Final Grade: 87/100 (B)

For an inexpensive, handmade, boxed cigar line just one step away from a no-name bundled smoke, this is a great cigar. It's not a big-time smoke, but it's a very pleasant "golf smoke" or low-cost supplement to bridge the gap between more expensive stogies. *Best Buy*

Dominican Olor (DOM)
Strength: Medium-mild
Appearance: 17/20 (B+)
Lighting & Burning: 13/15 (A-)
Construction: 26/30 (B)
Taste: 30/35 (B-)
Final Grade: 86/100 (B)

This well made cigar features good, smooth tobaccos. There isn't a lot of age behind Olor, but there isn't meant to be, nor is it priced as a great smoke. It's an excellent choice for an "everyday" cigar, or for something mild and pleasant on a weekend morning. *Best Buy*

Primo del Rey (DOM)
Strength: Mild
Appearance: 11/20 (D)
Lighting & Burning: 10/15 (B-)
Construction: 22/30 (D)
Taste: 24/35 (D)
Final Grade: 67/100 (D+)

Mottled wrappers and spongy construction get the cigar off on the wrong foot. The cigars have a somewhat strong and acrid quality, with a distinctive hay-like barnyard character. The flavor tends to improve toward the end, but they burn unevenly getting there.

Punch (HON)
Strength: Strong
Appearance: 19/20 (A)
Lighting & Burning: 14/15 (A)
Construction: 28/30 (A-)
Taste: 20/35 (D)
Final Grade: 82/100 (B+)

Punch gets you right at the base of your throat. This is a harsh, rough, strong cigar that will tickle burned-out taste buds and overwhelm normal palates. It is, however, incredibly well-made and consistent. It's loved by many and hated by many. It is not a subtle cigar. Obviously, my low score for taste reflects my own very negative opinion. Try one for the experience and form your own opinion.

Santa Clara (MEX)
Strength: Mild
Appearance: 18/20 (A-)
Lighting & Burning: 14/15 (A)
Construction: 27/30 (B+)
Taste: 29/35 (C+)
Final Grade: 88/100 (A-)

This is a relatively smooth-smoking and attractive cigar, considering it's all Mexican tobacco. There is a bit too much bitterness and tar toward the end, but it's one of the best Mexican-made smokes available. *Best Buy*

Te Amo (MEX)
Strength: Medium
Appearance: 17/20 (B+)
Lighting & Burning: 12/15 (A-)
Construction: 27/30 (B+)
Taste: 26/35 (C-)
Final Grade: 83/100 (B-)

This cigar is very consistently made at a reasonable price, but the Mexican tobacco is harsh. It's widely available with several wrapper styles. The maduro-wrapped cigar tastes a little sweeter than the natural wrapper. *Best Buy*

La Unica (DOM)
Strength: Mild
Appearance: 17/20 (B+)
Lighting & Burning: 13/15 (A-)
Construction: 26/30 (B)
Taste: 29/35 (C+)
Final Grade: 86/100 (B+)

Basically, this bundled cigar has been treated as a boxed cigar. It's a very nice cigar and certainly a good value. There's a tendency toward slightly spongy construction. It features an attractive Connecticut shade-grown wrapper and most sizes are available in maduro. A very good value. *Best Buy*

Vueltabajo (DOM)
Strength: Mild to medium
Appearance: 17/20 (B)
Lighting & Burning: 12/15 (B+)
Construction: 26/30 (B)
Taste: 25/35 (C)
Final Grade: 80/100 (B-)

This is a highfalutin' name for a cigar that has nothing to do with Cuba's Vuelta Abajo other than the Cuban seed tobacco it features, like most other non-Havana cigars. There's some harshness present.

Medium-Priced Cigars

Here are cigars for the slightly more willing spender—roughly in the $5 to $8 range. You'll find many a great smoke at a reasonable price here, and you won't have to hide your receipts!

Ashton (DOM)
Strength: Medium
Appearance: 18/20 (A-)
Lighting & Burning: 13/15 (A-)
Construction: 26/30 (B)
Taste: 33/35 (A-)
Final Grade: 90/100 (A)

The regular line of Ashtons is well constructed (by Fuente) and features silky Connecticut shade-grown wrappers. Occasionally these wrappers are so delicate that they crack when smoked. Ashtons also feature an excellent, sweet maduro wrapper on several sizes. The wrapper makes a considerable difference in flavor, but Ashton maduros are in very short supply. The line features a wide variety of sizes and usually burns well. The Cordial is one of the best small cigars around. *Great Smoke*

La Aurora (DOM)
Strength: Mild
Appearance: 15/20 (B-)
Lighting & Burning: 10/15 (B)
Construction: 22/30 (C-)
Taste: 22/35 (D)
Final Grade: 69/100 (C-)

This Cameroon-wrapped cigar once had a great reputation, but today the consistency is so highly variable that it cannot be listed among the contenders. The tobaccos consistently show signs of being too young. A positive sign is that family member Guillermo Lèon has made a major commitment to returning the La Aurora and Leon Jiminez brands to their former glory, and it will be very exciting if he succeeds.

Baccarrat (DOM)
Strength: Very mild
Appearance: 17/20 (B+)
Lighting & Burning: 13/15 (A-)
Construction: 25/30 (B-)
Taste: 32/35 (B+)
Final Grade: 86/100 (B+)

This cigar is very interesting with a very sweet taste that I'm sure is from naturally sweet cigar leaf rather than an artificial means. It's consistently well made, although it burns a little hot because the tobacco is a bit too loosely rolled. The wrappers are a little dry, but it's a very pleasant and interesting smoke. *Best Buy*

Belinda (HON)
Strength: Mild
Appearance: 15/20 (B-)
Lighting & Burning: 13/15 (A-)
Construction: 20/30 (D)
Taste: 22/35 (D)
Final Grade: 70/100 (C-)

A lot of smokers disagree with me on this cigar. I have not had much success finding consistently constructed, smooth-smoking Belinda cigars, but perhaps I'm looking in the wrong places. Belindas are deficient in quality, often showing spongy construction and rough wrappers. They tend to burn unevenly. The tobacco is green, albeit smokeable.

Caballeros (DOM)

Strength: Medium-mild
Appearance: 17/20 (B+)
Lighting & Burning: 12/15 (B+)
Construction: 22/30 (C-)
Taste: 28/35 (C)
Final Grade: 79/100 (B-)

Caballeros are generally well made with shade-grown wrappers, but they lack complexity in flavor and tend toward an overly tight draw. The aging of the filler tobaccos is somewhat inconsistent, but good enough to have attracted a loyal following. *Best Buy*

Casa Blanca (DOM)

Strength: Mild
Appearance: 18/20 (A-)
Lighting & Burning: 14/15 (A)
Construction: 26/30 (B)
Taste: 31/35 (B)
Final Grade: 89/100 (B+)

This is a nice-looking cigar that comes with both a very dark maduro and an attractive natural shade-grown wrapper. It's well-constructed and smooth-burning. If you're into really thick cigars, the line features the Jeroboam, an outrageous 10 inches with a 66 ring gauge (a 50 ring is the outer limits for most cigars) and a half Jeroboam at 5 inches by 66 ring that looks somewhat obscene. Mild and usually well-aged cigars, they have a somewhat bland flavor, but are still great, mild smokes. *Best Buy*

Cruz Real (MEX)

Strength: Medium to medium-full
Appearance: 14/20 (C+)
Lighting & Burning: 13/15 (A-)
Construction: 23/30 (C)
Taste: 28/35 (C)
Final Grade: 78/100 (B)

Typical of Mexican-made smokes, the Cruz Real line has somewhat dry wrappers and tastes like the tobaccos were not aged sufficiently. Among Mexican-made cigars, this relative newcomer seems like one of the best. I haven't smoked enough of them to judge long-term consistency.

Cuba Aliados (HON)

Strength: Full-bodied
Appearance: 19/20 (A)
Lighting & Burning: 14/15 (A)
Construction: 24/30 (C+)
Taste: 32/35 (B+)
Final Grade: 89/100 (A-)

The chocolate-brown EMS wrappers on these cigars are shiny, and the hard-to-find natural wrapper is nice, too. The supply of these smokes is spotty—and recent cigars I've seen have spotty wrappers, as well. The overall quality is good, but it may be degrading because of a shortage of leaf. The line features lots of sizes, including an excellent Churchill and hard-to-roll pyramid shape. Even burning and very smooth for a robust cigar, with no bitterness. The tobacco seems consistently well fermented and aged, and the price is very reasonable. If Cuba Aliados has a flaw, it's that too many cigars are too tightly rolled. *Great Smoke & Best Buy*

Cubita (DOM)

Strength: Mild
Appearance: 16/20 (B)
Lighting & Burning: 13/15 (A-)
Construction: 23/30 (C)

Taste: 27/35 (C)
Final Grade: 79/100 (B-)

This line offers a relatively mild but interesting smoke, slow and even burning until the final inch or two. If you toss the cigar with a couple of inches left, it would get a higher rating. However, I detected increasing harshness on some samples as the cigars burned past halfway, and a tendency to burn unevenly with a couple inches left.

Don Diego (DOM)
Strength: Mild
Appearance: 17/20 (A-)
Lighting & Burning: 15/15 (A+)
Construction: 30/30 (A+)
Taste: 32/35 (B+)
Final Grade: 94/100 (A)

This is an old-line brand and, amazingly to me, over-looked by many cigar smokers because it isn't new and sexy. I'll take established and consistent any day! Made by Consolidated Cigar Co. and overseen by the quality-conscious Richard DiMeola, it's a bastion of consistency. If there's a drawback, it's that the flavor is very mild and not particularly complex, but not every cigar has to knock your ears off. As a mild smoke, its Macanudo is equal at a much lower price. The line offers lots of shapes and sizes. The coffee-and-cream colored, natural shade-grown wrappers are a bit on the dry side, but are very consistent in color and quality. Only a couple of shapes come in maduro. *Great Smoke & Best Buy*

Don Juan (DOM)
Strength: Mild
Appearance: 17/20 (B+)
Lighting & Burning: 13/15 (A-)
Construction: 23/30 (C)
Taste: 20/35 (D)
Final Grade: 73/100 (C)

A lot of smokers like this cigar, but others complain it is both bland and bitter. It doesn't have a complex or interesting flavor, but the line does carry a reasonable price tag. The aging of the tobacco seems somewhat inconsistent. Don Diego, Baccarat, Macanudo, and Cuesta Rey are all better mild cigars.

Don Tomas (HON)
Strength: Very full-bodied
Appearance: 19/20 (A)
Lighting & Burning: 14/15 (A)
Construction: 28/30 (A-)
Taste: 18/35 (D)
Final Grade: 79/100 (B-)

This is a heavy, old-style Honduran line of cigars. Many smokers, including me, would call it harsh and strong, which it has always been. It's consistently well made with attractive dark wrappers, but the taste of the tobaccos shows signs of brief aging and is almost unpleasantly peppery. It's a favorite of some, but it isn't what I'd call a "polished" cigar. If you like a "rough and ready" stogie, you might like the Don Tomas line.

Dunhill Montecruz Sun Grown (DOM)
Strength: Medium
Appearance: 16/20 (B)
Lighting & Burning: 14/15 (A)
Construction: 26/30 (B)
Taste: 31/35 (B)
Final Grade: 87/100 (A-)

This cigar offers dark, sun-grown, natural wrappers, which have a slightly stronger and more vegetal, asparagus flavor than shade-grown wrappers. (This flavor isn't bad, but it is unique.) The Montecruz line occasionally can be a little harsh and the wrappers are inconsistent, ranging from oily to dry. It does have a unique flavor, however, and thus represents a true change of pace in your cigar-smoking repertoire. *Best Buy*

Fonseca (DOM)
Strength: Medium
Appearance: 19/20 (A)
Lighting & Burning: 14/15 (A)
Construction: 28/30 (A-)
Taste: 33/35 (A-)
Final Grade: 94/100 (A)

This brand, which has a marketing tie-in with Fonseca port, took off like a rocket in the early 1990s and never looked back. There's a Cuban Fonseca, so don't get the two confused. Interestingly, people seem to either love it or hate it, and some smokers find it harsh, but I haven't noticed this trait. I would say the line shows body and some spice. To smokers of mild cigars, the Fonseca is too heavy. For those who like full-bodied cigars, this is a milder alternative that still shows character. The triangular is one of the most reasonably priced pyramids available, and it's very well made. Recently, I've had a few Fonsecas that show signs of green tobacco and tend toward some bitterness, but I'm hoping that with a top-notch maker like Manuel Queseda at the helm, this cigar will remain great. *Great Smoke & Best Buy*

La Fontana (HON)
Strength: Medium-full
Appearance: 15/20 (B-)
Lighting & Burning: 12/15 (B+)
Construction: 25/30 (B-)
Taste: 27/35 (B)
Final Grade: 81/100 (B-)

There's nothing distinguishing about this brand, except for the sizes named after great Italian artists, musicians, and scientists.

Arturo Fuente Chateau and Double Chateau (DOM)
Strength: Medium-full
Appearance: 19/20 (A)
Lighting & Burning: 13/15 (A-)
Construction: 28/30 (A-)
Taste: 34/35 (A)
Final Grade: 94/100 (A)

Most smokers don't know this, but these two cigars, one a
Rothschild and the other a double Rothschild, have a different, spicier blend than the regular Fuente line. The
Rothschild, or robusto, is one of the best on the market,
packing a lot of punch in a short smoke. Rothschilds are
individually wrapped in cedar, which accentuates the cedar flavor they get from spending time in Fuentes' cedar-
lined aging room. They come in a natural Connecticut
shade-grown wrapper and a hard-to-find maduro wrapper.
Great Smoke & Best Buy

Hoyo de Monterrey Excalibur (HON)
Strength: Full
Appearance: 18/20 (A-)
Lighting & Burning: 14/15 (A)
Construction: 28/30 (A-)
Taste: 33/35 (A-)
Final Grade: 93/100 (A)

The Hoyo Excalibur line is easy to distinguish from regular
Hoyos by the label, which says "Excalibur" and Roman
numeral sizes I through VII. This cigar is full-bodied, but
the tobacco is well fermented and aged and very smooth.
Both the English claro and maduro wrappers are attractive. Even the smaller Excaliburs are tasty and smooth.
More expensive than the regular Hoyo line, the Excalibur
is still an excellent value. *Great Smoke & Best Buy*

Joya de Nicaragua (NIC)
Strength: Medium
Appearance: 15/20 (B-)
Lighting & Burning: 12/15 (B+)
Construction: 27/30 (B+)
Taste: 22/35 (D)
Final Grade: 76/100 (C+)

This was once a fine line, but the civil war of the 1970s and 1980s virtually destroyed the tobacco fields. Joya has always relied heavily on Nicaraguan tobacco, and while the fields are beginning to recover, there isn't enough supply of aged leaf to fill these cigars. They're generally harsh cigars, without much complexity.

Leon Jiminez (DOM)
Strength: Full
Appearance: 14/20 (C+)
Lighting & Burning: 11/15 (B)
Construction: 23/30 (C)
Taste: 20/35 (D)
Final Grade: 68/100 (C-)

Made by La Aurora, this brand exhibits the same inconsistency of tobacco you'll find in La Aurora. This is a very heavy cigar, but also bitter, with lots of tar. Here's hoping Guillermo Lèon can return the line to former glory.

JR Ultimate (HON)
Strength: Full-bodied and robust
Appearance: 19/20 (A)
Lighting & Burning: 14/15 (A)
Construction: 25/30 (B-)
Taste: 31/35 (B)
Final Grade: 89/100 (A-)

This cigar is heavy but smooth. It had some quality-control problems for a couple years, particularly related to the loss of Honduran leaf to blue mold, but returned

to its former quality and consistency a few years ago.
Now, it seems as if the exclusive retailer, Lew Rothman of
JR Cigars, cannot get enough leaf to even begin to keep up
with demand for the Ultimate. The line offers a multitude
of sizes and wrappers, including jade. *Best Buy*

Jose Llopis (PAN)
Strength: Medium-full
Appearance: 18/20 (A-)
Lighting & Burning: 13/15 (A-)
Construction: 23/30 (C)
Taste: 28/35 (C)
Final Grade: 82/100 (B)

It's hard to find this line, which features good cigars at
reasonable prices. Well constructed, with a tendency to be
too firm, the line features somewhat dry wrappers and an
even draw.

Licenciados (DOM)
Strength: Medium-mild
Appearance: 18/20 (A-)
Lighting & Burning: 12/15 (B+)
Construction: 25/30 (B-)
Taste: 26/35 (C)
Final Grade: 81/100 (B)

Individual cigars in this line have received some high ratings in cigar publications, which I don't agree with. While
it's a tasty, reasonably priced line, it can't compete with
the top brands. It tends to be harsh due to underage tobaccos. It can be very good, and has developed a devoted
following, but if it were more consistent, it would be a
much better cigar. It features a Dominican filler, Honduran binder, and consistently average to dry Connecticut
shade-grown wrapper. It lacks complexity, but is a good
value, burns evenly, and is reliable and pleasant as an
"everyday" smoke. *Best Buy*

New York (MEX)
Strength: Medium
Appearance: 17/20 (B+)
Lighting & Burning: 12/15 (B+)
Construction: 23/30 (C)
Taste: 24/35 (D)
Final Grade: 76/100 (C+)

This is a sub-brand of the Te Amo line, and the cigars are pleasant, average Mexican smokes. I feel like my bias against Mexican cigars is showing, but I find the taste somewhat harsh.

Onyx (DOM)
Strength: Medium
Appearance: 15/20 (B-)
Lighting & Burning: 12/15 (B+)
Construction: 25/30 (B-)
Taste: 25/35 (C-)
Final Grade: 77/100 (C+)

With its black oscuro wrapper, this cigar has created quite a sensation among maduro lovers and has developed a regular following. Today's shortage of maduro leaf makes it harder than ever to have a brand that features only maduro wrappers. The wrappers are relatively dry, especially for maduro, and not as naturally sweet as the best maduro leaves. The cigar frequently burns unevenly, but the flavor is very consistent from beginning to end, and there's no tar buildup. It tends to taste stale, and the aroma to those around you is also pungent and slightly stale. Still, smokers whose taste I respect enjoy the Onyx, so you may just have to try this cigar and decide for yourself.

Partagas (DOM)
Strength: Medium
Appearance: 18/20 (A-)
Lighting & Burning: 14/15 (A)
Construction: 27/30 (B+)
Taste: 33/35 (A-)
Final Grade: 92/100 (A)

This brand from General Cigar (which also makes Macanudo) has been, like Macanudo, a time-tested standard of quality and consistency. It's a nice choice because it has character and complexity, and it's one of the few lines still using the Cameroon wrapper, which has been hard to get in recent years. Because of this supply problem, some Partagas wrappers have looked a bit "shaggy" in the past, but wrapper quality seems to be improving. The cigar has a rich taste, yet isn't robust, which gives those who don't enjoy a "heavy" cigar the chance to enjoy the sensation of a full-bodied smoke. Some of the cigars exhibit squaring due to box pressure. *Great Smoke & Best Buy*

Petrus (HON)
Strength: Medium-full
Appearance: 18/20 (A-)
Lighting & Burning: 13/15 (A-)
Construction: 25/30 (B-)
Taste: 28/35 (C)
Final Grade: 84/100 (B+)

I haven't sampled and observed as many of these as I would like in order to judge the entire line. The ones I have smoked are moderately complex and a bit vegetal, but the tobacco seems well aged. I have heard complaints about spongy construction, and burning is a little uneven but acceptable.

Primo del Rey Club Selection (DOM)
Strength: Mild
Appearance: 16/20 (B)
Lighting & Burning: 12/15 (B+)
Construction: 23/30 (C)
Taste: 28/35 (C)
Final Grade: 78/100 (B-)

This series, with a white, red, and gold band, is distinctly better than the regular Primo brand. There is still a bit of the barnyard about the Club Selection, and it still burns somewhat unevenly due to spongy construction.

Ramon Allones (DOM)
Strength: Medium
Appearance: 12/20 (C-)
Lighting & Burning: 13/15 (A-)
Construction: 27/30 (B+)
Taste: 25/35 (D)
Final Grade: 77/100 (C+)

This brand has been around for a while, but I sense under-age tobacco and some consistent harshness. The wrappers are relatively dry and unattractive. There's nothing particularly striking, good or bad, about this brand.

Royal Jamaica (DOM)
Strength: Mild
Appearance: 17/20 (B+)
Lighting & Burning: 13/15 (A-)
Construction: 27/30 (B+)
Taste: 31/35 (B)
Final Grade: 88/100 (A-)

When this brand was produced by the Gore family in Jamaica, it was one of my favorites. It featured a secret flavoring process that gave Royal Jamaicas a unique taste. When the Gore's factory was completely destroyed by Hurricane Hugo, the brand was sold to General Cigar

Company, and production shifted to the D.R. The cigars just don't taste the same. They're still pleasant and mild, however, and an enjoyable smoke. They offer a maduro wrapper, but all Royal Jamaica look a bit rough and dry. *Best Buy*

Saint Luis Rey (HON)
Strength: Medium
Appearance: 20/20 (A+)
Lighting & Burning: 13/15 (A-)
Construction: 27/30 (B+)
Taste: 30/35 (B-)
Final Grade: 90/100 (A)

This relatively new entry is yet another brand using the name of a classic Havana cigar. It's a tasty smoke, and the line so far seems very consistent. If this continues, it could be a long-term winner. *Great Smoke & Best Buy*

Sosa (DOM)
Strength: Medium
Appearance: 14/20 (C+)
Lighting & Burning: 12/15 (B+)
Construction: 22/30 (C-)
Taste: 25/35 (C-)
Final Grade: 73/100 (C)

Spongy construction is the biggest downfall of this brand. Veiny, poorly constructed wrappers detract from the appearance. This brand seems to exhibit inconsistent fermentation and aging of tobaccos.

Signet (DOM)
Strength: Mild
Appearance: 18/20 (B+)
Lighting & Burning: 12/15 (B+)
Construction: 28/30 (A-)
Taste: 31/35 (B)
Final Grade: 89/100 (A-)

This new entry from Lane Limited, which has a solid reputation for consistency, is very tasty, with interesting spice
for an essentially mild cigar. Given the manufacturer's
decades-long commitment to quality, this could be a
winner. *Best Buy*

Tressado (DOM)
Strength: Mild
Appearance: 17/20 (B+)
Lighting & Burning: 13/15 (A-)
Construction: 27/30 (B+)
Taste: 29/35 (C+)
Final Grade: 86/100 (B+)

With a pretty Indonesian wrapper and mild but interesting filler tobaccos, Tressado is a very affordable everyday
smoke. Its mild but engaging flavor is great if you're just
starting out with cigars. *Best Buy*

Troya (DOM)
Strength: Mild to medium
Appearance: 18/20 (A-)
Lighting & Burning: 14/15 (A)
Construction: 28/30 (A-)
Taste: 28/35 (C)
Final Grade: 88/100 (A-)

Introduced as a premium boxed cigar at a bundle cigar
price, Troya has succeeded in that it's a fine and pleasant
smoke. The blend and construction is very consistent. The
tobaccos are nicely fermented, but the cigar seems a little
short in the final aging and marrying. *Best Buy*

H. Upmann (DOM)
Strength: Medium
Appearance: 20/20 (A+)
Lighting & Burning: 14/15 (A)
Construction: 28/30 (A-)
Taste: 32/35 (B+)
Final Grade: 94/100 (A)

The Upmann used to feature a great Cameroon wrapper, but the shortage and inconsistent quality of Cameroon prompted the maker, Consolidated Cigar Company, to switch to an attractive Indonesian wrapper. The taste isn't quite the same, but H. Upmann remains a standard of consistency and reliability. It never turns tarry or bitter, and is widely available at an exceptionally reasonable price. *Great Smoke & Best Buy*

Chapter 11

Pricey Cigars

These cigars are more on the pricey side, somewhere in the $6.50 to $12 range, but hey, you're worth it!

Ashton Cabinet Selection (DOM)
Strength: Medium
Appearance: 19/20 (A)
Lighting & Burning: 13/15 (A-)
Construction: 26/30 (B)
Taste: 32/35 (B+)
Final Grade: 90/100 (A)

The Cabinet Selection line is good, using more aged tobaccos than the regular Ashton line, which lends a smoother character. They sometimes display uneven burning characteristics. They are perhaps not worth the difference in price. *Great Smoke*

Borhani (COS)
Strength: Medium to medium-full
Appearance: 20/20 (A+)
Lighting & Burning: 7/15 (C-)
Construction: 20/30 (D)
Taste: 22/35 (D)
Final Grade: 69/100 (C-)

Assembled in Costa Rica, the Borhani incorporates tobaccos from several countries. It's a great-looking cigar with a simple but eye-catching yellow band. The cigar tends to burn unevenly, however, which is a great disappointment because the wrappers are gorgeous, dark, and oily. The tobaccos inside are young, and become sharp and bitter during smoking. It apparently lacks the aged leaf necessary to be a great smoke. It could improve and mellow with a couple of years in your humidor, but aging won't help the construction.

Credo (DOM)
Strength: Medium
Appearance: 18/20 (A-)
Lighting & Burning: 14/15 (A)
Construction: 27/30 (B+)
Taste: 31/35 (B)
Final Grade: 90/100 (A)

Since being introduced a few years ago, this cigar seems to have maintained a high level of quality and consistency. It has a complex and interesting flavor, excellent construction, and pleasant greenish-brown Connecticut shade-grown wrappers. The cigars feature offbeat names like Arcane and Pythagoras. *Great Smoke*

Diana Silvius (DOM)
Strength: Medium
Appearance: 19/20 (A)
Lighting & Burning: 14/15 (A)
Construction: 28/30 (A-)
Taste: 33/35 (A-)
Final Grade: 94/100 (A)

This cigar is well made, with good body and relatively complex taste. It has a cedar resonance from marrying time in cedar aging rooms. *Great Smoke*

Don Lino, Don Lino Habano Series, Don Lino Colorado Series (HON)

Strength: Medium-mild
Appearance: 19/20 (A)
Lighting & Burning: 11/15 (B)
Construction: 24/30 (C+)
Taste: 25/35 (C-)
Final Grade: 79/100 (B-)

This line has rapidly grown in popularity since its introduction a few years ago, but I find all of the Don Lino cigars to smoke somewhat harsh, hot, and bitter. Even the Colorado and Habano Reserve lines, which feature different blends and use more vintage tobacco, are somewhat harsh. Because so many people like them, I strongly suggest you try them for yourself.

Don Tomas Special Edition (HON)

Strength: Medium
Appearance: 13/20 (C)
Lighting & Burning: 14/15 (A-)
Construction: 28/30 (A-)
Taste: 30/35 (B)
Final Grade: 85/100 (B+)

The five sizes in the special edition line are very different in flavor and strength from the regular Don Tomas. The special edition line is relatively mild and well-constructed. It's a bit harsh, but it's still an interesting cigar because it combines a mild smoke with that dryish, peppery, Honduran cigar-making style. The natural wrappers can be incredibly blotchy and unattractive, but some are smooth and creamy. Inconsistency earns a slap on the knuckles with teacher's ruler, and the score and grade gets lowered.

Dunhill (DOM)
Strength: Medium
Appearance: 19/20 (A)
Lighting & Burning: 13/15 (A-)
Construction: 29/30 (A)
Taste: 32/35 (B+)
Final Grade: 93/100 (A)

This is a flavorful, medium-bodied line using well-aged tobaccos and featuring only natural wrappers. The line includes Dunhill Dominicans as well as Dunhill Canary Island cigars, which are assembled in the Canary Islands. The Canary Island smokes are supposedly milder, in the Canary Island tradition, but I can't tell a difference. The Dunhill line offers several tubed selections, good for gifts and traveling. Dunhills strike a nice balance between lengths and ring gauges, creating very attractive cigars with a preponderance of larger ring gauges (48 to 50). Although they are very well made and even-burning, some smokers find they lack a degree of character and complexity. They used to be pricey, but everyone else has caught up to them and Dunhill now represents a decent value. *Great Smoke & Best Buy*

8-9-8 Collection (DOM)
Strength: Medium
Appearance: 18/20 (A-)
Lighting & Burning: 11/15 (B)
Construction: 23/30 (C)
Taste: 26/35 (C-)
Final Grade: 78/100 (B-)

I've noticed an unpleasant, slightly metallic taste throughout the smoke. The construction of the cigars tends toward spongy, but the overall draw is good and the burn rate is reasonably even. I've noted signs of lack of aging in the filler tobaccos.

Flor de Florez Cabinet Selection (DOM)
Strength: Medium to medium-full
Appearance: 18/20 (A-)
Lighting & Burning: 13/15 (A-)
Construction: 26/30 (B)
Taste: 32/35 (B+)
Final Grade: 89/100 (A-)

This line is a step up from the regular Flor de Florez, and uses some very nice, aged tobaccos. Because it's a relative newcomer, I wonder whether it can maintain the quality it now shows. I hope so, because the wrappers are attractive and relatively oily, and the cigar is well constructed with a smooth, even draw. *Great Smoke*

Arturo Fuente Hemingway Series (DOM)
Strength: Medium-mild
Appearance: 20/20 (A+)
Lighting & Burning: 15/15 (A+)
Construction: 28/30 (A-)
Taste: 34/35 (A)
Final Grade: 97/100 (A+)

With an impeccable Cameroon wrapper, the cigars in this series exhibit the height of the cigar-roller's art with a tapered foot and head: the classic and seldom-found "perfecto" shape. If anything, the cigars are occasionally rolled too lovingly and tightly, so the draw can be a little firm. The lush "Masterpiece" (9 inches by 52 ring) is a celebratory cigar at a very reasonable price. *Great Smoke & Best Buy*

Arturo Fuente Don Carlos Reserve Series (DOM)
Strength: Full-bodied
Appearance: 19/20 (A)
Lighting & Burning: 15/15 (A+)
Construction: 28/30 (A-)
Taste: 34/35 (A)
Final Grade: 96/100 (A+)

Although the selection of sizes in this line is extremely limited, as is supply, the cigars show the usual excellent Fuente construction. The robusto is excellent. *Great Smoke*

Gispert (DOM)
Strength: Medium
Appearance: 18/20 (A-)
Lighting & Burning: 13/15 (A-)
Construction: 25/30 (B-)
Taste: 31/35 (B)
Final Grade: 87/100 (A-)

This cigar is only available to smoke shops that are members of a special tobacconists association. If you patronize a shop that carries it, you'll find a very nice, smooth line of cigars that uses well-aged tobaccos and is well constructed. It's a good smoke at a reasonable price. *Best Buy*

The Griffin's (DOM)
Strength: Mild
Appearance: 16/20 (B)
Lighting & Burning: 12/15 (B+)
Construction: 25/30 (B-)
Taste: 30/35 (B-)
Final Grade: 83/100 (B)

The lack of large ring sizes in this brand is frustrating if you like the smoking characteristics of a thicker cigar. Most Griffin's run 38 to 44 ring gauge. Some smokers find the cigar bland, but as a mild cigar, I think it's complex and interesting. My favorite is the Prestige. At 8 inches by 48 ring, it's a good value. Construction of the line is good, but the natural shade-grown wrappers are inconsistent and sometimes papery. I've even come across the rare, reddish tan, and oily colorado rosa wrappers on this brand.

Thomas Hinds (HON)
Strength: Medium-full
Appearance: 18/20 (A-)
Lighting & Burning: 12/15 (B+)
Construction: 25/30 (B-)
Taste: 30/35 (B)
Final Grade: 86/100 (B+)

When this cigar first came out, it was one of the least expensive premium smokes around, and it was delicious. I bought boxloads, which I'm still enjoying. (See why it pays to have a humidor?) The introductory price was raised, and the quality and consistency of the filler tobaccos seem to have diminished slightly in the past couple years. Still, the Hinds features a good range of standard sizes and nice, thick ring gauges on all sizes. The line has a smooth natural Ecuadorian wrapper, double binder, and primarily Honduran filler. The cigars burn evenly, and although they are Honduran, they aren't strong or peppery. The line is worth your while to try to find it.

Thomas Hinds Nicaraguan Selection (NIC)
Strength: Medium
Appearance: 17/20 (B+)
Lighting & Burning: 13/15 (A-)
Construction: 27/30 (B+)
Taste: 26/35 (C-)
Final Grade: 83/100 (B-)

Among the blended cigars being made with primarily Nicaraguan tobaccos, this line is consistently well made and has nice, subtle flavors. It tastes a little rough and dry, however. It might improve with aging; the tobaccos seem a little short on finished aging but generally seem well-fermented.

Macanudo (JAM/DOM)
Strength: Mild
Appearance: 19/20 (A)
Lighting & Burning: 14/15 (A)
Construction: 28/30 (A-)
Taste: 33/35 (A)
Final Grade: 94/100 (A)

The country of assembly is listed as Jamaica, famed for mild stogies, but much of the tobacco is Dominican. The Macanudo line is one of the most consistent, well-constructed brands you'll find. Many veteran smokers think they're far too bland, but if you enjoy mild cigars, or occasionally feel like a break from heavier cigars, this is a great smoke from General Cigar Co. Macanudos come in a huge variety of shapes, a few with a maduro wrapper option, but most with Connecticut shade-grown wrappers. The small Ascots ($4^1/_8$ inches by 32 ring) are great small smokes, while large sizes such as the Prince Philip ($7^1/_2$ inches by 49 ring) are good values. Value in the rest of the line depends on the particular shape. *Great Smoke & Best Buy*

Montecristo (DOM)
Strength: Medium
Appearance: 18/20 (A-)
Lighting & Burning: 13/15 (A-)
Construction: 24/30 (C+)
Taste: 31/35 (B)
Final Grade: 86/100 (B+)

This new introduction is yet another effort to borrow classic Havana names and use them in non-Havana cigars. It's a good-looking line, with a bit of spice. The samples I've tried burned somewhat unevenly. Time will tell whether this brand can maintain consistency.

Nat Sherman (DOM/HON)

Strength: Mild to robust
Appearance: 18/20 (A-)
Lighting & Burning: 14/15 (A)
Construction: 28/30 (A-)
Taste: 33/35 (B+)
Final Grade: 93/100 (A)

This brand, sold primarily through the Nat Sherman store in Manhattan, is tough to rate because the line contains cigars with different tastes and strengths. I've smoked many different Shermans, and they're consistently well made and delicious, from mild to the most robust. Like everything in New York, the cigars are expensive.

Oscar (DOM)

Strength: Medium full
Appearance: 19/20 (A)
Lighting & Burning: 12/15 (B+)
Construction: 27/30 (B+)
Taste: 30/35 (B)
Final Grade: 88/100 (A-)

This cigar straddles the border between smooth sophistication and a peppery Cuban-style pizzazz. The flavor is nicely balanced and the tobaccos are consistent. Its aroma is pungent, so smoke these only with cigar-loving friends. It's an attractive brand with a Connecticut shade-grown wrapper.

Por Larranaga (DOM)

Strength: Medium-mild
Appearance: 18/20 (A-)
Lighting & Burning: 14/15 (A)
Construction: 26/30 (B)
Taste: 28/35 (C)
Final Grade: 86/100 (B+)

This is a re-creation of the classic Cuban extolled by Rudyard Kipling in a famous poem. Wrapped individually in cedar with a gold band and pretty shade-grown wrapper, it makes a beautiful impression. However, I have found the brand shows some harshness and signs of insufficient aging.

Punch Gran Cru (HON)
Strength: Full-bodied
Appearance: 19/20 (A)
Lighting & Burning: 14/15 (A)
Construction: 28/30 (A-)
Taste: 33/35 (A-)
Final Grade: 94/100 (A)

The Gran Cru series is an entirely different creature from the regular Punch line. You have to be careful when you buy to look for the special bands—either a Punch band combined with a miniature Honduran cigar tax seal, or a red-and-gold Punch label with a black stripe at the bottom. The blend of high-quality Honduran, Dominican, and Mexican tobaccos is subtle and reflects thorough fermenting and aging. It's a beautifully constructed cigar and is consistent box after box. The Gran Cru is also an excellent value. *Great Smoke & Best Buy*

Santa Damiana (DOM)
Strength: Medium-mild
Appearance: 18/20 (A+)
Lighting & Burning: 13/15 (A-)
Construction: 28/30 (A-)
Taste: 27/35 (C-)
Final Grade: 86/100 (B+)

This brand has generated a lot of excitement since its introduction a few years ago. It's beautifully made with smooth Connecticut shade-grown wrappers. I find it's a little bitter and harsh, especially toward the end. It could be slightly underage tobacco, but it's still a good smoke.

Temple Hall (DOM/JAM)

Strength: Mild
Appearance: 20/20 (A+)
Lighting & Burning: 14/15 (A)
Construction: 29/30 (A)
Taste: 31/35 (B)
Final Grade: 94/100 (A)

This is the café latte of cigars: smooth, rich, and creamy. It's one of the best mild cigars available, yet exhibits a level of complexity that's unusual for a mild cigar. The construction is consistent and excellent and the wrappers are attractive silky shade-grown Connecticut leaf. Some Temple Hall sizes are also available with an attractive sweet maduro wrapper. This cigar ages well and improves in richness and complexity after a year or two in the right conditions. The belicoso shape is expensive but offers incredible oily, silky wrappers. Temple Hall has been an East Coast favorite for years, and is being discovered (slowly) by the rest of the country. If you can find it, Temple Hall is probably one of the finest mild cigars you're likely to find. *Great Smoke*

V Centennial (HON)

Strength: Medium-full
Appearance: 19/20 (A)
Lighting & Burning: 14/15 (A)
Construction: 28/30 (A-)
Taste: 28/35 (C)
Final Grade: 89/100 (A-)

Although made in Honduras, the V Centennial is less robust than many Hondurans due to blended tobaccos from the Dominican Republic. It features smooth Connecticut shade wrappers. It lacks some complexity, but it's a pleasant smoke and offers a pretty torpedo shape. *Great Smoke & Best Buy*

Zino (HON)
Strength: Medium to full-bodied
Appearance: 18/20 (A-)
Lighting & Burning: 12/15 (B+)
Construction: 28/30 (A-)
Taste: 31/35 (B)
Final Grade: 88/100 (A-)

This is a spicy, Honduran-style cigar that isn't overpowering, yet is relatively robust. The wrappers are a little dry and the average ring sizes are relatively thin (34 to 44). The line offers a nice panatela, if you like thinner cigars. The tobacco is well aged and the cigars never turn harsh or bitter. The foil-wrapped Classic Brazil and Classic Sumatra offer different tobacco tastes, if you enjoy Brazilian and Sumatran tobaccos.

Chapter 12

Trés Pricey Cigars

Okay, these are the cigars your mother warned you about. They run in the $10 to $25 range, but as you'll see, many of them are truly great smokes. If you want to indulge yourself with a rare treat once in awhile—or if you want a cigar as expensive as the single-malt scotch you'll be sipping with it—then scan through this chapter for the ones to try.

Avo Uvezian Regular and XO Series (DOM)
Strength: Robust
Appearance: 20/20 (A+)
Lighting & Burning: 15/15 (A+)
Construction: 29/30 (A)
Taste: 34/35 (A)
Final Grade: 98/100 (A+)

This is a beautifully constructed cigar. The natural wrappers are usually luscious and oily. The line offers the unusual belicoso, petit belicoso, and pyramid shapes. The XO is purported to use more aged tobaccos, but I don't notice much difference in flavor between the two lines. Then again, I don't know how you can improve much on the regular Avo line. The cigar is manufactured by Hendrik Kelner, one of the world's finest cigar makers. The cigars are subjected to many quality control checks, and I've never seen a bad one. Being a full bodied cigar, it isn't for the faint of heart, but it's always smooth, made with vintage tobaccos. *Great Smoke*

Butera (HON)
Strength: Full-bodied
Appearance: 20/20 (A+)
Lighting & Burning: 14/15 (A)
Construction: 27/30 (B+)
Taste: 32/35 (B+)
Final Grade: 93/100 (A)

This robust cigar is consistently well made using attractive, smooth colorado claro wrappers. Some smokers say they detect bitterness, but I never have, and I've smoked many Buteras. I do notice a faint, almost seaweed resonance, which is not at all unpleasant. Mike Butera is a world-class U.S. pipe maker, and his cigars reflect a commitment to quality. Made in limited quantities, they're tough to find, but worth the hunt. *Great Smoke*

Juan Clemente (DOM)
Strength: Medium-full
Appearance: 19/20 (A)
Lighting & Burning: 14/15 (A)
Construction: 23/30 (C-)
Taste: 23/35 (D)
Final Grade: 79/100 (B-)

This cigar features a band applied to the foot of the cigar instead of the usual placement near the head. It's beautiful looking, but I find that these cigars become very tarry and bitter halfway through the smoke, which is inexcusable for a premium cigar.

Davidoff Nos. 1-3, Aniversario and 2, Ambassadrice (DOM)
Strength: Medium-mild
Appearance: 20/20 (A+)
Lighting & Burning: 15/15 (A+)
Construction: 30/30 (A+)
Taste: 33/35 (A)
Final Grade: 98/100 (A+)

Davidoff produces several lines of cigars featuring differ-ent blends. These cigars are the mildest of the Davidoff series, but still have a lot of body and flavor. In price-weighted ratings, Davidoff cigars get downgraded because of their extremely high price—they are one of the most expensive smokes available. Price aside, every aspect of every Davidoff is nearly perfect because of high-quality tobacco, good construction, and meticulous quality control. The natural, Connecticut shade-grown wrappers are excellent and consistent in color and quality within each box, but will vary considerably from box to box—from olive green to a rich colorado rosa. Most wrappers are oily and silky. *Great Smoke*

Davidoff 1000 Series (DOM)
Strength: Medium
Appearance: 20/20 (A+)
Lighting & Burning: 15/15 (A+)
Construction: 30/30 (A+)
Taste: 33/35 (A)
Final Grade: 98/100 (A+)

The entire Davidoff line is made by Hendrik Kelner, who also manufactures two of the world's other great smokes, Avo Uvezian's Avo and Paul Garmirian's PG. This Davidoff series offers a little spice and a medium body you expect to find only in more robust cigars. Filler tobaccos are well aged and mature. To my mind, the major flaw (other than price) in this series is that most ring gauges in the Davidoff line are thinner than I like (30 to 42) to get sufficient smoke volume. Only the #5000, at 5^1/$_2$ inches by 46 ring, has a satisfactory circumference. *Great Smoke*

Davidoff Gran Cru Series (DOM)

Strength: Medium-full
Appearance: 20/20 (A+)
Lighting & Burning: 15/15 (A+)
Construction: 30/30 (A+)
Taste: 34/35 (A)
Final Grade: 99/100 (A+)

As far as the rating goes, second verse same as the first! Although fuller than other Davidoffs, the smokes in this series are not what you'd call robust, but they do have body and very pleasant spice. This series was developed as the Dominican alternative to Davidoff's discontinued Cuban line, and it upholds the tradition. The quality is impeccable but, once again, I find the ring gauges of the five sizes (40 to 42) too thin. The cigars' length-to-width balance is close to perfect. *Great Smoke*

Davidoff Special and Double "R," Special "T," and Tubo (DOM)

Strength: Robust
Appearance: 20/20 (A+)
Lighting & Burning: 15/15 (A+)
Construction: 30/30 (A+)
Taste: 34/35 (A)
Final Grade: 99/100 (A+)

These are the fullest-bodied cigars offered by Davidoff—and my favorites. The ring gauges of these three are wider, allowing more smoke volume. The Special R (5^1/$_2$ inches by 50 ring) is a superb robusto, the Double R (7 inches by 52 ring) is excellent, and the Special T is one of the best pyramid shapes you'll find. The Tubo is a bit thin at 6 inches by 38 ring, but each comes in a white tube and is wrapped in cedar and makes a nice gift. *Great Smoke*

El Sublimado (DOM)
Strength: Mild
Appearance: 19/20 (A)
Lighting & Burning: 14/15 (A)
Construction: 28/30 (A-)
Taste: 33/35 (A-)
Final Grade: 94/100 (A)

Made for Hardy Cognac in the Dominican Republic, this is an interesting cigar because the leaf is cured in rooms with Hardy cognac. (The cognac is not applied directly to the leaf.) This is the only premium cigar cured with fine spirits, but there's barely a hint of the brandy. There's also a single-malt whiskey-cured El Sublimado, the flavor of which is very faint. The spirit's smell on the unsmoked wrappers is more pronounced than in the actual smoking. The construction is excellent, and most of the natural wrappers are rich and oily, but some are papery. The El Sublimado line offers several sizes. It's an extremely expensive smoke, and if you can't taste much cognac flavor, it's a lot to pay for a mild cigar. *Great Smoke*

Fuente Fuente OpusX (DOM)
Strength: Robust and full-bodied
Appearance: 20/20 (A+)
Lighting & Burning: 15/15 (A+)
Construction: 26/30 (B)
Taste: 35/35 (A+)
Final Grade: 98/100 (A+)

If you like a very spicy, powerful, Cuban-style cigar, the Fuente Fuente OpusX fits the description. It's well made, using very aged tobacco with noticeable hints of cedar aging. The construction can occasionally be overly firm, but the cigar is made with high levels of consistency and care. The cigar has a large band that must be removed to finish the cigar, so be careful not to tear the dark, oily, Dominican-grown EMS wrapper. It's a hard-to-find and expensive smoke, but is one of the heartiest Cuban-style cigars you'll encounter. *Great Smoke*

La Gloria Cubana (US)
Strength: Medium to full
Appearance: 15/20 (B-)
Lighting & Burning: 11/15 (B)
Construction: 24/30 (C+)
Taste: 27/35 (C)
Final Grade: 77/100 (C+)

This line isn't one of my highest-ranking brands for one reason: The caliber of the tobaccos is hopelessly inconsistent. If he gets good leaf, manufacturer Ernesto Carillo can make one of the best cigars around. I've had La Glorias that were like a dream and others that were a nightmare of green tobaccos. That's why the taste rating for the brand is so low. It used to be an inexpensive smoke and worth the risk of an occasional bad stogie, but it has become both expensive and hard to find, taking away any advantage it once enjoyed.

Macanudo Vintage Collection (JAM/DOM)
Strength: Mild to medium
Appearance: 19/20 (A)
Lighting & Burning: 14/15 (A-)
Construction: 28/30 (A-)
Taste: 31/35 (B)
Final Grade: 92/100 (A-)

This line offers a distinctly heartier flavor than the regular Macanudo line. It comes with a super-premium price, and it isn't on a par with some of the other smokes in its price league. While its tobaccos are well-aged, the blend isn't very interesting or complex.

PG/Paul Garmirian (DOM)

Strength: Robust
Appearance: 19/20 (A)
Lighting & Burning: 15/15 (A+)
Construction: 30/30 (A+)
Taste: 35/35 (A+)
Final Grade: 99/100 (A+)

Another product of Hendrik Kelner's Dominican factory (like Davidoffs and Avos), every PG exhibits the relentless quality control of Kelner and its creator, Paul Garmirian. It's a robust, spicy, Havana-style brand and is extremely consistent and beautifully constructed. Production is very limited, and the brand isn't widely distributed. It was the first line to offer the tapered-tip Belicoso, a shape that's now all the rage among smokers. The PG "Bom-Bones" ($3^1/2$ by 43) has won acclaim as one of the best small cigars made. The ring gauges are thick to maximize smoke volume. Despite being robust, the cigar smokes smooth. The shade-grown wrappers are excellent. This is one of the finest brands available. Although it's expensive, the price is reasonable compared with other super-premium smokes, given the quality and consistency. *Great Smoke*

Padron 1964 Anniversary Series (NIC)

Strength: Medium
Appearance: 17/20 (B+)
Lighting & Burning: 13/15 (A-)
Construction: 26/30 (B)
Taste: 20/35 (D)
Final Grade: 76/100 (C+)

This line, featuring all Nicaraguan tobacco, has received a lot of acclaim since its recent introduction. I think it shows signs of green tobacco and harshness, and there's a distinct damp-wood flavor I didn't like. This is a good example of a cigar I'd like to try several times in the future to make a better assessment.

Pleiades (DOM)
Strength: Mild
Appearance: 18/20 (A-)
Lighting & Burning: 12/15 (B+)
Construction: 23/30 (C)
Taste: 31/35 (B)
Final Grade: 84/100 (B+)

This is a pleasant, mild cigar with some complexity.
The binder and filler exhibit fine and consistent construction, but the thin shade-grown wrappers tend to crack and unravel.

Romeo y Julieta Vintage (DOM)
Strength: Mild to medium
Appearance: 20/20 (A+)
Lighting & Burning: 14/15 (A)
Construction: 29/30 (A)
Taste: 31/35 (B)
Final Grade: 94/100 (A)

From the initial appearance of the silky, shade-grown
Connecticut wrappers to the final draw on a small stub,
this cigar bespeaks quality. It is always in short supply, for
good reason. It has been the immediate favorite of many
smokers since its introduction a few years ago. There is
subtle spice, yet the cigar is still mild. *Great Smoke*

Savinelli Extra Limited Reserve (DOM)
Strength: Medium to full
Appearance: 20/20 (A+)
Lighting & Burning: 15/15 (A+)
Construction: 29/30 (A)
Taste: 33/35 (A-)
Final Grade: 97/100 (A+)

This cigar is superior in every way. The line features hearty
tobaccos with a bit of spice and very consistent appearance and flavor. If you enjoy this cigar, whose namesake is

a top-line Italian pipe maker, you will enjoy it time and again because the line maintains the highest quality control. *Great Smoke*

Great Smokes and Best Buys

Great Smokes

Ambassadrice
Ashton
Ashton Cabinet Selection
Avo Uvezian Regular and XO Series
Butera
Canaria D'Oro
Credo
Cuba Aliados
Davidoff 1000 Series
Davidoff Gran Cru Series
Davidoff Nos. 1–3, Aniversario 1 and 2
Davidoff Special and Double "R"
Diana Silvius
Don Diego
Dunhill
El Sublimado
Flor de Florez Cabinet Selection
Fonseca

Arturo Fuente Chateau and Double Chateau
Arturo Fuente Don Carlos Reserve Series
Arturo Fuente Hemingway Series
Fuente Fuente OpusX
H. Upmann
Hoyo de Monterrey Excalibur
Macanudo
Partagas
PG/Paul Garmirian
Punch Gran Cru
Romeo y Julieta Vintage
Saint Luis Rey
Savinelli Extra Limited Reserve
Special "T" and Tubo
Temple Hall
V Centennial

Best Buys

Baccarrat
Caballeros
Canaria D'Oro
Casa Blanca
Cuba Aliados
Cuesta Rey
Dominican Olor
Don Diego
Dunhill
Dunhill Montecruz Sun Grown
Fonseca
Arturo Fuente Chateau and Double Chateau
Arturo Fuente Hemingway Series
Arturo Fuente Regular Line
Gispert
H. Upmann
Hoyo de Monterrey Excalibur
JR Ultimate

La Unica
Licenciados
Macanudo
Montesino
Partagas
Punch Gran Cru
Royal Jamaica
Saint Luis Rey
Santa Clara
Signet
Te Amo
Tressado
Troya
V Centennial

Great Smokes/Best Buys

Canaria D'Oro
Cuba Aliados
Don Diego
Dunhill
Fonseca
Arturo Fuente Chateau and Double Chateau
Arturo Fuente Hemingway Series
H. Upmann
Hoyo de Monterrey Excalibur
Macanudo
Partagas
Punch Gran Cru
Saint Luis Rey
V Centennial

Cigar Speak Glossary

8-9-8 packaging   This refers to cigars that are packed in a box three layers deep, with nine cigars in the middle and eight on the top and bottom rows.

aging   Storing stogies under humidified conditions for extended periods of time. Many cigar makers combine cigars for several months before shipping to allow the tobacco to "rest" and the flavors to blend. Individuals can also age cigars in humidors. Subtle mellowing can develop with aging.

air curing   The process of hanging freshly picked tobacco leaves in open-air, covered barns to dry in the breeze. This allows the flavors of the tobacco to concentrate, and the unwanted chemicals to dissipate. (See also *heat curing*.)

bales   After tobacco leaves have finished fermenting, they are packed up in a bale made from the tough sheath of the palm tree and encased in burlap, which provides a home for the leaves while they age, and also serves to transport them safely.

band   A colorful strip of paper applied around the cigar, usually near the head, that identifies the maker.

binder   A leaf of tough, coarse tobacco that holds the filler tobacco in place, which is then covered by a leaf of wrapper tobacco.

blending   Most cigars are blended, which means manufacturers use tobaccos from all over the world to achieve the desired balance of flavor and strength.

body   See *strength.*

box pressure   Certain cigars are pressed so tightly into a box that they assume a slightly square shape. Most premium cigars are carefully packed into boxes to retain their original round shape.

boxes   Cedar cigar boxes are generally called *boite nature,* which is French for "natural box." There are also a variety of paper-covered cardboard and basswood boxes.

bunchers   Some cigar factories use employees who specialize in assembling the "guts" of premium cigars and wrapping them in a binder. Bunchers are often apprentice rollers, or less skilled than full-fledged rollers.

bundled cigars   Sometimes cigars are sold in bundles of 10 or 25, rather than in a box. Bundling and wrapping in plastic saves money, so less expensive smokes, or "seconds," are bundled. Bundled cigars can be a good deal.

cap   See *flag.*

cedar   Cedar can impart a delicate and pleasing woody flavor to tobacco. Cedar is used to make cigar boxes, and to line the walls of humidors and cigar aging rooms.

chavetta (or **tuck**)   A specialized crescent-shaped knife that is one of the cigar-roller's only tools. It's used to cut the leaf, pack the filler into the cigar, and shape the stogie.

cheroot   A small cigar. A century ago, cheroots were often smoked using a decorative holder.

cigar bar   A place with comfortable seating and/or tables where you can buy individual cigars and accompany them with drinks.

cigar drill   A type of cutter. See also *pinhole cutter.*

cigarillo   A "small cigar," generally not much bigger than a cigarette. It's made from cigar-leaf tobacco, but due to its small size, it generally contains short filler to promote proper, even burning.

climate   A critical part of growing good cigar leaf. Even slight differences in temperature and rainfall will make the same type of tobacco plant have a different flavor.

cohiba   A variation of the term for tobacco used by natives of the Caribbean hundreds of years ago. The word *cohiba* was used to name Cuba's best and most famous brand of cigar—which was created for Fidel Castro.

color   Refers to the shade of the leaf used to wrap your cigar, which can range from light green to almost jet black. All shades have specialized names, such as natural, colorado, or maduro.

consistency   The hallmark of a premium cigar brand, meaning that almost every cigar you buy over the weeks, months, and years will be well constructed, use properly aged tobaccos, and feature almost identical wrapper colors within a box (for visual appeal).

curing   See *air curing.*

cutter   A device used to remove or puncture the cap of tobacco used to seal the tip of a cigar. There are numerous types of cutters, and several styles of cuts.

debudding   The process of nipping off the flower buds that sprout from the top of a tobacco plant, forcing the plant to expend all its energy to grow bigger, better leaves.

fermentation When air-cured tobacco leaves are placed in large piles and allowed to heat up, the process is called fermenting, bulking, or sweating the tobacco. Tobacco fermentation is basically highly controlled composting, and releases many chemicals and impurities that would otherwise ruin the tobacco's flavor.

fillers See *long filler* and *short filler*.

flag or **cap** The head of a premium cigar is covered by a "flag" of tobacco, which is carefully applied at the end of the cigar-rolling process. If applied properly, the flag is smooth, feels good in your mouth, and helps prevent the wrapper from unraveling.

foot The business end of the cigar—the end that you light.

free zone An area of a country specifically set aside to receive shipments of foreign products—the only place where free movement of non-domestic materials is allowed. Because of free zones, Caribbean-based cigar makers can legally import tobaccos and other materials for use in creating their smokes.

handmade cigar A cigar created primarily by individuals, not machines.

head This is the end you smoke. It's covered by a piece of tobacco, called a "flag," or "cap."

heat curing Accelerating the natural drying process of tobacco using heat. Without sufficient time for flavors to concentrate, this process results in a leaf with less flavor and richness than air-cured leaves.

homogenized tobacco product Pulverized and reconstituted tobacco blended with natural binders. It's used as the wrapper for a number of cigarillos.

humidor An enclosed device that keeps cigars in a tropical climate. A humidor can be a huge walk-in room, a box made of wood or Plexiglas, or something as simple as a sealed plastic bag—anything that maintains the relatively high level of airborne moisture, or humidity, cigars require to keep from drying out.

hygrometer A device used to read and measure humidity levels.

length The length of your cigar is measured in inches or millimeters.

long filler Long-filler cigars are filled with long leaves of tobacco.

machine-made cigar A cigar made primarily by a machine. The filler in most machine-made cigars is short filler, or tobacco scraps.

nicotine This chemical, in its pure state, is colorless and highly poisonous. It also has the characteristic smell of tobacco. Tobacco contains a very small percentage of nicotine, and cigar leaf contains among the smallest amount of nicotine of all tobacco. Only about 2 percent of the leaf's content is nicotine.

packing Premium cigars come packed in two ways—square pack and round pack. All handmade cigars are round when they're made, and a round pack preserves this shape. Some cigars are pressed into a box so tightly that they take on a square shape.

pinch test An easy way to check the construction of your cigar is to lightly "pinch" the cigar between your thumb and index finger. It should feel firm, but not hard. If it feels like a piece of wood, or if you feel a soft, spongy spot, choose a different cigar.

pinhole cutter (or **cigar drill**) A cutter that creates a small airhole in the head of the cigar through which you draw smoke.

premium or **super-premium cigar**   This is a cigar made by hand and worthy of praise because it's a brand that's consistently excellent from one cigar to the next and from box to box.

puncture cutter   This type of cutter, when inserted into the head of a cigar, removes a plug approximately $1/4$ inch across, creating a large air hole while still preserving the smooth, rounded head of the cigar.

ring gauge   Measures the thickness of a cigar in $1/64$-inch increments. A 32-ring cigar would be a half inch in diameter.

rollers   Experienced rollers apply the cigar wrappers. In some tobacco factories, a few master rollers apply wrappers only. In other factories, rollers are responsible for making entire cigars.

scissors cutter   This cutter looks like a pair of scissors, but with special blades for cutting a cigar. It delivers a straight cut.

seconds   Cigars that are rejected by manufacturers for a variety of reasons are frequently sold as "seconds." They are often packaged economically, and sold at a significant discount to the company's firsts. The flaws, however, may be so insignificant that the seconds represent an excellent value.

shape   The shape of a cigar is the length balanced with a particular ring gauge. Some standard combinations of length and ring gauge exist—such as corona or robusto.

short filler   The middle of a short-filler cigar is filled with scraps of tobacco, rather than long leaves. Virtually all short-filler cigars are made by machines.

sizes   Cigars are classified by their length and girth, or ring size. There are certain combinations of length and girth that are standard, and many of these have special names. Three examples are the robusto (short and thick); the corona (moderately slim and in the middle of the cigar length spectrum); and the double corona, sometimes called a Churchill, which is long and relatively thick.

straight or **guillotine cut**   This most common of all cuts lops off the head of a cigar in a straight, clean line, allowing air to be drawn through the cigar. A straight cut can be made using a cutter with one blade, or two blades.

strength or **body**   The relative strength or body of your cigar means whether it's mild, medium, or full-bodied.

stripping   Stripping tobacco means removing the thick stem that attaches the tobacco leaf to the stalk. After the stem is stripped, the tobacco leaf dies, and its growth process essentially stops.

tercio   A burlap-wrapped bale (about the size of a hay bale) containing aged individual tobacco leaves. The tercio is used to protect and transport the tobacco, and also to store the tobacco during the aging process.

tobacciana   A general term that refers to smoking-related collectibles and memorabilia. From advertisements to books to six-foot cigar-store Indians, tobacciana includes an almost unlimited variety of items.

tobacco plant   The tobacco plant is divided into three basic sections. The top leaves, which comprise the corona, are small and somewhat harsher because of their exposure to the sun. The lower leaves are called volado, and they burn well and have higher nicotine content. The prized middle leaves are the largest, and are called seco.

tobacconist   A tobacconist is distinguished from a mere cigar retailer by several things: a wide selection of brands and sizes; proper humidification for the stock; a strong working knowledge of cigars, tobacco, and brands; and a selection of smoking-related accessories such as cutters, lighters, and humidors.

v-cut   A top-to-bottom slice that creates a v-shaped wedge through the head of the cigar.

Vuelta Abajo   Roughly pronounced *voo-el-tah ah-bah-o,* this region of Cuba is the world's most famous cigar leaf-growing real estate.

wrapper   A silky leaf of tobacco that makes your cigar look and feel attractive.

young or **green tobacco**   Tobacco that has been insufficiently cured, fermented, and aged. Proper processing removes many chemical compounds that make tobacco harsh and strong. Smoking even the best tobaccos, without proper maturation and mellowing, will make you sick.

Index

E-F-G

H-I-J-K

T-U-V

W-X-Y-Z